JULIE GOODWIN

The heart of the home

JULIE GOODWIN

The heart of the home

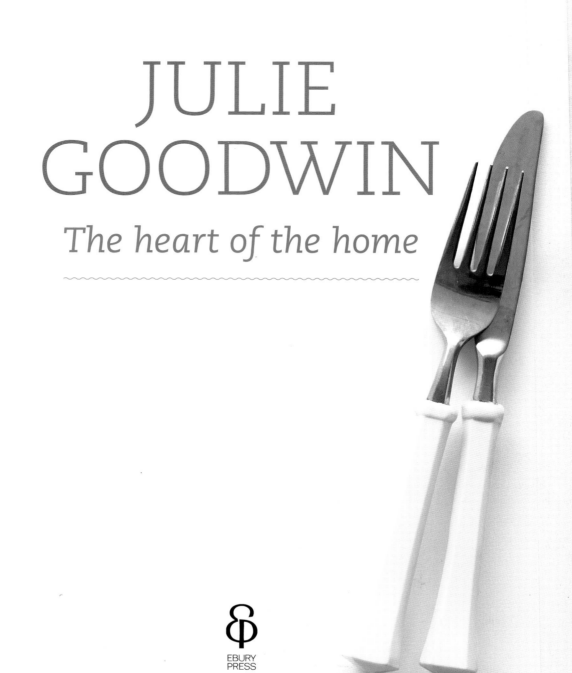

EBURY
PRESS

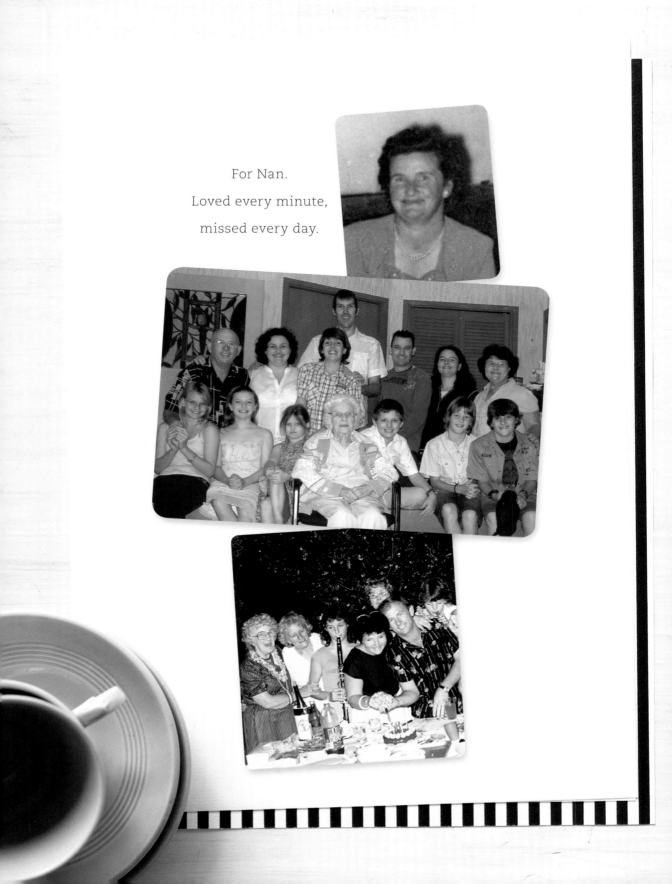

For Nan.
Loved every minute,
missed every day.

Contents

Author's note

Occasionally in this book I recommend the use of a chef's pan. This is similar to a large frying pan, but it has straight, deep sides. Mine is 32 cm across and 7.5 cm deep. When cooking for a large number of people (or teenagers!) it's very handy, and I would recommend investing in one if you can.

When I refer to shallots I mean the long green onions that are sometimes called spring onions or eschallots. I do not mean the little brown French shallots.

When I refer to icing mixture, it is the fine white powder that is very similar to icing sugar.

Butter is unsalted unless otherwise specified.

Eggs are large (59 g) and free range.

It's my commitment to you that ingredients used in my recipes are accessible to most Australians. We have such a wonderful and diverse range of ingredients available to us, even in our supermarkets, so this is not a restrictive commitment.

I try wherever possible to source my food locally. This is for a number of reasons. Food that has been grown in the area is likely to be fresh and is definitely seasonal. It won't have been in cold storage for months and will not only eat better but will keep better than produce that has been stored.

Another reason is that it hasn't been transported far. An orange picked off the tree in the backyard has had no adverse effect on the environment, as opposed to an orange that has been freighted from the US. The same goes for local meats, eggs, cheeses, smallgoods . . . It can be quite an adventure to find out what is produced in your local area. Not everyone can grow their own vegies and keep their own chooks, but the growers' markets in your area are one great source of fresh local goods.

When using any recipe, it is important to remember that there can be a huge variation in equipment, temperatures and results. The size of the pan or cake tin, the heat on the stove or in the oven, even the air temperature can impact cooking results. In my recipes I try to describe how the food should look, taste, smell or behave at various stages. I encourage you to use these clues as well as temperature time.

I hope that beginning cooks can step out these recipes and enjoy success. I hope that more experienced cooks can draw inspiration and then fly off on a tangent. I hope that parents can get their kids into the kitchen. I aim to make cooking as enjoyable and achievable as possible. Get into it and enjoy!

Introduction

A funny thing happened to me a few weeks go. I was at the wedding of Mick's young cousin, Jessica. It was the first wedding we had attended in a few years, since his sister Liz's wedding in fact, and something pretty huge had shifted in me in the intervening years.

When I looked at the brothers of the bride, and the groomsmen, and listened to the speeches, I was seeing my own children. For the first time, instead of identifying myself as a peer of the bride and groom, I identified myself as a peer of the parents.

I started to think about this young couple starting their lives, creating the heart in their own home . . . It was a wonder a fiddler didn't appear on the roof and start playing 'Sunrise Sunset'.

It was a strange feeling, to be able to easily imagine my own sons standing up there making their wedding speeches. It gave me the sensation of a huge wheel turning, of a picture much bigger than I had previously given thought to.

I am sure everyone has felt this passage of time at some moment or another. Maybe it's when you look at a photo of one of your children that was only taken recently but they have changed so much. Or when you run into an old friend you haven't seen in a long time and note the differences in them (changes that surely haven't happened in you?). Or, as in my case, you look through your wedding album and realise that a significant proportion of the guests present on that day are no longer alive. Maybe (like me) it's when you look in the mirror and realise that if you keep pulling out all the white hairs on your head you will end up half bald.

It has been quite a confronting transition for me to make. I know we get older, and so do our kids. I know it's our role as parents to raise our kids to be happy, well-adjusted adults. So, if that is what's happening, why do I feel like grieving instead of rejoicing? The bigger and more independent they get, and the closer we are to achieving our parental goals, the further they grow from our lives.

So, what happens when I can no longer compel them to be home for dinner, or for Christmas, or their birthdays? What happens when I don't get to see them or speak to them every day? I have to admit to occasionally getting myself into quite a state over this.

Then, like a bolt of wisdom from the blue (or more likely from my nan in heaven), I realise that I am no longer compelled to share my family's Christmas table either. And yet I do. Mick is a grown man now, and is not obligated in any way to be involved in the lives of his extended family. And yet, he is. Both of us still remain tied to the people who have been around us our whole lives.

Why is that? It can't just be obligation, or guilt. Those things aren't enough to hold a family together.

When we gather with our families, there's always so much laughter. We enjoy each other! So besides family obligation, I think the secret of the continued contact is that it's not a chore to get together – it's fun. I believe that the great times shore us up, too, for the challenges that life throws at us every now and again, challenges that often must be faced as a family.

And, of course, these gatherings always revolve around a great meal, usually one that everyone has contributed to in one way or another.

All families are different and I have had the great honour of being allowed glimpses into many diverse lives during the writing of this book. Talking to people about food, about their memories, their experiences and beliefs has been the most deeply rewarding part of this whole process.

I got some insight from the children in the family – my own, Joe, Tom and Paddy; along with my sister Debbie and Kieron's four, Sam, Luke, Lauren and Jess; Paul and Lyn and their children, Jamie, Brie, Kirsten and Hayden. Mick's other brothers and sisters also shared more of their great family memories – Anthony and Andrea, whose Chinese recipes are in the book; Liz and Steve, Bec and Ben. I can't wait until Lucy, Finlay, Mason and Audrey are big enough to give me their opinions about their family's traditions and foods.

Mick's aunts and cousins also contributed, especially Saul, Terese, Lesley and Pauline. Erin, Trudy, Michelle and Treen, along with the whole book club, sent me reams of great information and recipes. Friends Louise, Kelly, Mary, Rose,

Josh, Alison and Marcus also delved into their memory archives. Even more quips, quotes and dishes came from Adam, Dan, Steph, Tash, Jackie and Pete.

I got some wonderful insights about growing up in South Africa and the food there from Martin and Mandy, Nikki and Wade; some fabulous Greek philosophy and recipes from Maria and Liane; and some Lebanese traditions from Francine.

We have been fortunate enough to travel a little as well. I have been especially inspired by the vibrant colours and flavours of India, and the fresh, fabulous simplicity of Vietnamese food. Those experiences and the things I learned have made their way into my repertoire and into this book. As I tend to do, I have adapted them so that, while still evoking their country of origin, they are able to be made with ingredients available to most of us.

Every person I spoke with and everywhere I went, I asked: who, or what, is the heart of your home? Of course, the old adage is that the kitchen is the heart of the home. But the answers that came back were far more diverse and interesting than that. You will find them throughout the pages of this book.

For me, the heart of the home is my family. The kitchen is simply the hub of our family activity – it's where we most often gather to eat, where the boys usually find me, where all the best goodies come from. So, while the family is the heart of the home, the kitchen is where we dwell. (Maybe you could say the kitchen is the rib cage of our home, but it lacks a certain romanticism.)

So, life goes on. And running through the generations like a bright thread are the common values that hold us together. From the time we humans crouched around fires in our caves until today, and hopefully for ages to come, the basics haven't changed. We are born, we grow, we gather together and celebrate; we feast and dance and tell stories; we laugh and we mourn and we wonder.

In the scheme of things, we are alive for really what is only a brief, shining time. I have no memory of my ancestors from only three generations ago. But my memories of my nan are so fiercely, dazzlingly strong that they bring tears to my eyes. I am grateful with every breath that I had such a person in my life.

The heart of Nan's home was Nan – and what a heart. She loved this country. She was fiercely patriotic and always championed the little Aussie battler. She would stop strangers in the street for a 'mag', and she called everyone mate. She laughed easily and frequently, and loved a McWilliams Cream Sherry (which she bought by the flagon for economy).

Nan was determined that no special occasion would be marred by an argument, and she believed that being together was more important than all the riches in the kingdom. She pedalled the old pianola until well into her 80s and sang along with gusto.

Other childhood memories of Nan include her faded rose wallpaper and cowhide rug; the mint growing wild through the cracks of the concrete path; and her big banana trees that only ever gave little bananas. I remember her making a tent with the bedsheets when I stayed the night, and giving me salvaged office paper and fat carpenter's pencils to draw with.

Nan loved her husband with a single-minded intensity and absolute loyalty from the time they met until her passing at age 90 – even though he passed away almost 50 years before she did.

Her lasting legacy is that she passed those values on to all of us so that we, too, can experience a life fully lived.

Nan's life inspires me to play my part in the big picture, and to keep my loved ones close.

Whoever or whatever the heart of your home is, whether it is your kitchen, your backyard, your loved ones, yourself – my wish for you is that it is warm and inviting, and memorable, and filled with good things.

1 | The perfect sunday

Nature abhors a vacuum (so do I, Nature, so do I). In the same way, the calendar abhors a Sunday with nothing scheduled. If there ever is a free weekend, it seems to get taken over very quickly with kids' activities, school and sport events, not to mention the domestic duties that there are no time for in the week.

So, if I see an opening in the calendar I will often nab it and schedule in a relaxing day – what my teenage sons call a 'chillaxin' day'. This can take any number of forms but my favourite is going to Mass, then heading home to prepare a feast, and finally enjoying a lazy afternoon on the back deck. Whether this is with a group of friends, or family, or just the five of us, it is perfect.

I wanted to know what others do on their 'perfect Sunday', so I asked a huge number of people from the different circles in my life. The answers varied from sleeping in, to breakfast and brunches, going to the beach, fishing, playing sport (or watching it!), daytime naps, picnics, and taking time to read a book. (Nobody nominated ironing or making lunches for the coming week, oddly enough.) The overwhelmingly dominant answer was – the perfect Sunday involves a barbecue with friends.

This chapter offers recipes for many of the 'perfect Sunday' scenarios, but does focus mostly on the barbecue. According to my not very scientific research, it seems to be the most popular choice for celebrating the great outdoors, our wonderful friends, our abundant and beautiful food, and, most of all, a Sunday that is ours to do with as we wish.

Shakshuka

serves 4

Preparation time: 5 minutes
Cooking time: 20 minutes

This Middle Eastern dish consists of a rich, spicy tomato sauce, with eggs softly poached in it. With a crusty baguette and a good cup of coffee, it is an amazing brunch.

1 tbs olive oil	2 x 400 g tins chopped tomatoes
2 small red chillies, deseeded and finely chopped	1 tbs sugar
2 garlic cloves, chopped	2 tsp salt
1 brown onion, chopped	4 eggs
1 tsp ground cumin	⅓ cup chopped flat leaf parsley
1 tsp smoked paprika	ground black pepper

1 Heat the oil in a 28 cm frying pan over medium heat. Add the chillies, garlic and onion and stir until soft and translucent. Add the cumin and paprika and stir for a further minute.

2 Add the tomatoes, sugar and salt, and simmer for 10 minutes. The sauce will be thickened and the flavours intense.

3 Carefully crack the eggs into the sauce, spacing them evenly apart. Partially cover with a lid and simmer for a further 5 minutes, or until the whites have set and the yolks are still soft. Remove from the heat, sprinkle with parsley and season with pepper. Serve it at the table in the pan, with a crusty baguette. Delicious!

'The perfect Sunday – eggs and coffee after a sleep in, then to the beach for a swim, fish and chips, and a lazy afternoon with a good book.' – Erin

Banana pecan bread

serves 6–8

Preparation time: 10 minutes

Cooking time: 1 hour

I have tried to work out why banana bread is called that, and not banana cake. It really is a moist, lovely loaf cake. I think that it's probably because you can eat bread for breakfast, but you have to wait for morning tea to eat cake. And you won't want to wait to eat this.

3 very ripe bananas	¾ cup (150 g) brown sugar *or caster*
125 g butter, melted	1½ cups (240 g) wholemeal self-raising flour *or s/r white flour*
2 eggs, beaten	¼ teaspoon ground cinnamon
1 tsp vanilla essence	1 cup (120 g) pecans, chopped *or choc chip or walnuts or both*

1 Preheat the oven to 180°C (160°C fan-forced). Grease and flour a medium (4-cup capacity) loaf tin.

2 Mash the bananas well in a large bowl. Add the butter, eggs, vanilla and sugar and combine thoroughly. Fold through the flour and cinnamon, then add the pecans.

3 Pour the batter into the loaf tin and bake for an hour *50min to* until risen, dark golden and coming away from the edges of the pan. A skewer inserted into the centre of the bread should come out clean, but this is a very moist, dense loaf. Cool in the tin for 10 minutes before turning out onto a wire rack to cool.

Note: This is delicious on its own, but to turn it into the ideal breakfast or brunch dish, serve it warm with a generous dollop of plain yoghurt, some slices of fresh banana and a drizzle of honey.

'Best Sunday ever is a sleep-in, a swim and watching the footy with Dad. Especially a Tigers game. Especially if they win.' – Paddy

Peach and ginger jam

makes about 2 cups

Preparation time: 20 minutes
Cooking time: 45 minutes

In the summertime peaches are sold by the box – inexpensive, in season and gorgeous.
It's a great time to make a batch of this lovely preserve.

1.5 kg (approx 10) peaches, just under-ripe
3 cups (660 g) white sugar

2.5 cm piece fresh ginger,
peeled and cut into thin strips

1 Score a cross into the base of each peach. Place into a large heatproof bowl and cover with boiling water. Stand for 2 minutes, then drain. Cool slightly, then slip off the skins. Remove the stones and coarsely chop the flesh.

2 Place all the ingredients into a large saucepan. Bring to the boil over high heat, stirring constantly until sugar has dissolved. Skim off any scum that rises to the surface.

3 Reduce heat to low and continue to boil until jam thickens and reaches 220°C on a sugar thermometer. Another way to test if the jam is ready is to spoon a little onto a cold plate and place into the freezer for a few minutes. If it stays thick and jammy and does not run, it is set. Spoon into sterilised jars; seal and cool.

Note: Serve on sourdough toast for a divine, easy Sunday morning brekky.
Most recipes for preserves tell you to put them into sterilised jars. There is no special equipment needed for this – put them through the hot cycle on the dishwasher, or place them on a tray in the oven at 180°C for 10 minutes. Allow them to cool down before filling.

'A chillin' summer's day at home is my perfect Sunday.' – Joe

'Toasted bacon and banana sandwiches are a common breakfast in Durban, where I grew up.' – Mandy

Whole barbecued baby snapper

serves 4

Preparation time: 10 minutes
Cooking time: 15–20 minutes

We holiday on the South Coast of NSW, and often watch the fishing boats come in
from the sea with their catch. There's a table where they pull in and clean the fish
they have caught, before throwing the scraps to the waiting seals and enormous manta rays.
It's quite spectacular. Here is one recipe that could be used for those beautiful fresh fish.

½ bunch flat leaf parsley, leaves roughly chopped
2 garlic cloves, chopped
1 lemon, zested, fruit thickly sliced
½ cup (80 g) pine nuts
2 tbs olive oil

¼ tsp ground black pepper
salt
2 whole baby snapper, cleaned and scaled
  (about 500 g each)
fresh lemon wedges, to serve

1   Preheat a hooded barbecue – turn the outside burners on and leave the middle ones off.
    Alternatively, preheat an oven to 180°C (160°C fan-forced). In a mortar and pestle, combine
    the parsley, garlic, lemon zest, pine nuts, half the olive oil, the pepper and a pinch of salt,
    and pound to a thick paste.

2   On the bench, lay out a large piece of extra-wide foil (or two normal-sized pieces folded to join in the
    middle). Cover this with extra-wide baking paper (or two normal pieces folded to join in the middle).
    Place a snapper in the middle of one of the paper sheets and score deeply 3–4 times on each side.
    Work half of the pine nut paste into the cuts and place lemon slices into the cavity. Repeat with the
    second fish. Drizzle the remaining oil over the two fish. Gather the paper and foil around each fish
    to form parcels that are loose but which have no gaps in the joins.

3   Place onto the middle plates of the barbecue (the ones with no direct heat under them). Cook for
    about 15–20 minutes. The cooking time will depend on a number of things – how many times
    you open the barbecue to check it, the thickness of the fish and the temperature of the outside air.
    To check, carefully open the foil at the top and, prodding with a fork, see if a small piece of the fish
    at the thickest part moves easily away from the bone.

4   Serve the fish with any reserved juices and some fresh lemon wedges on a platter and allow diners
    to help themselves. When all the flesh on top of the skeleton has been served, lift the skeleton off
    to allow access to the lovely soft flesh underneath.

Chermoula-marinated king prawns

serves 4

Preparation time: 10 minutes + 15 minutes marinating
Cooking time: 5 minutes

To cook prawns with good colour and tender flesh, the key is to make sure the plate
or pan is hot enough, and not to overcrowd them or they will stew and be tough.

½ bunch fresh mint, leaves finely chopped
½ bunch flat leaf parsley, leaves finely chopped
½ large bunch coriander, leaves finely chopped
2 garlic cloves, finely chopped
1 small brown onion, finely chopped
finely grated zest of ½ lemon

1½ tsp ground cumin
¼ tsp ground black pepper
1 kg green king prawns, peeled and deveined,
   tails intact
1 tbs vegetable oil
salt

1 Combine all the ingredients except for the prawns, oil and salt, and mix well. Place into a snap-lock bag with the prawns. Seal tightly and gently massage through the bag to coat the prawns evenly. Refrigerate for 15 minutes.

2 Remove the bag from the fridge and heat the flat plate of the barbecue to high. Drizzle the oil onto the hotplate and when it is smoking, put the prawns on. Turn carefully after a couple of minutes and cook for a further minute. Depending on the size of the prawns, they will take 2–3 minutes to cook through.

3 Remove when still very slightly underdone as they will keep cooking for a few moments after being removed. Season with salt and some extra ground black pepper. Serve with crusty bread.

'Basic barbecue wisdom – food over heat cooks. Food over flame burns.' – Dan

'My perfect Sunday is on the beach, swimming, beach cricket and sausages on bread.' – Nic

Barbecue rack of lamb
with pistachio crumble

serves 4

Preparation time: 20 minutes + 30 minutes marinating
Cooking time: 15 minutes

When I was growing up, lamb was the cheapest meat. These days it's among
the most expensive, and a bit of a treat, so I like to give it some special treatment
when I am buying premium cuts like the rack.

3 garlic cloves, crushed
finely grated zest and juice of 1 lemon
2 tbs olive oil
black pepper

4 x 4-cutlet racks of lamb, trimmed
⅓ cup (45 g) pistachios, roughly chopped
½ cup (20 g) coarse fresh breadcrumbs
salt

1 Combine 2 of the garlic cloves, the lemon zest, and 2 teaspoons of the olive oil in a large bowl.
   Season with freshly ground black pepper. Put the lamb racks into the marinade and massage to
   ensure the meat is coated. Set aside for 30 minutes.

2 In a non-stick frying pan, toast the pistachios over medium heat until lightly browned and fragrant;
   set aside. Heat 1 tablespoon of the olive oil and sauté the breadcrumbs until crisp and golden.
   Season with salt and pepper. Combine with the pistachios and set aside.

3 Wrap the exposed bones of the cutlets with aluminium foil to prevent them from burning. Rub
   the meat with a little oil, and season with salt and pepper. Grill on a medium-high barbecue for
   about 10 minutes, turning occasionally, or until cooked to your liking. Rest under foil for 5 minutes
   before serving.

4 Remove the foil from the racks and carve very carefully into double chops. Scatter generously with
   the crumble.

   Note: This is especially delicious served on a bed of sautéed spinach, asparagus and shallots.

Balsamic grilled vegetables

serves 4

Preparation time: 10 minutes
Cooking time: 10 minutes

The beauty of this dish is it can be varied according to what
vegies you have in the house or garden.

1 eggplant, sliced 1 cm thick
2 zucchini, sliced lengthways, ½ cm thick
2 red onions, peeled, base intact, cut into wedges
1 bunch asparagus, trimmed
1 bunch broccolini, trimmed
4 large flat mushrooms, sliced

2 tbs olive oil
salt and ground black pepper
¼ cup (60 ml) orange-infused balsamic glaze
   (see next page) or store-bought balsamic glaze
½ cup flat leaf parsley, chopped
½ cup basil leaves, chopped

1   Preheat a barbecue grill to medium-high.

2   Brush the vegetables with olive oil and cook on the grill plate until char-marked and softened
(around 10 minutes, but you may need to cook in batches depending on space).

3   Transfer to a tray and season with salt and pepper. Toss with balsamic glaze and scatter with
fresh herbs.

*'The perfect Sunday afternoon for me is playing golf with my wife, hitting a winning
score, a few drinks with friends at the 19th, followed by a good meal.' – Tony*

Orange-infused balsamic glaze

makes 400 ml

Preparation time: 5 minutes
Cooking time: 1 hour

The addition of orange peel to the reducing balsamic glaze gives it a beautiful
depth of flavour which makes it lovely on grilled vegetables, and meats, and in salads.

rind ½ orange   ½ cup (110 g) caster sugar
4 cups (1 litre) balsamic vinegar

1   Using a vegetable peeler, cut the rind from the orange in long strips, avoiding the white pith.

2   Bring the vinegar, sugar and orange rind to the boil in a medium saucepan. Reduce the heat and
    simmer for an hour or until thickened and reduced by about half.

3   Allow to cool, then strain into a sterilised jar or bottle.

    Note: This will create an unholy smell in the house so be sure to open the windows!

*'One of my most firmly held food beliefs is, "don't come home late and drunk and
then put a meal on the stove and go to bed". My brother used to do this and it made
a real mess of the kitchen.' – Tony*

Our wedding day – my mum, dad and nan, Mick's mum,
grandpa and grandma celebrate with us.

'One Mother's Day we invited my mum, Jules' mum and sister,
and all the family to our place for a celebration lunch. We had
to bring the outdoor setting indoors to fit everyone at the table,
which Jules set beautifully. She made the most enormous baked
dinner – it was great. Happy Mother's Day, Jules!' – Mick

Aussie hamburgers

makes 4 burgers

Preparation time: 15 minutes + 15 minutes chilling
Cooking time: about 15 minutes

These are the old-fashioned corner store style hamburgers.
Add egg, bacon and a pineapple slice for 'one with the lot'!

For the patties	For the burger
500 g premium beef mince	1 large brown onion, sliced
1 egg	4 hamburger buns, split
½ cup (40 g) grated parmesan cheese	4 slices tasty cheese
2 large garlic cloves, crushed	1 cup (250 ml) burger sauce (see overleaf),
½ cup (20 g) fresh breadcrumbs	or tomato or barbecue sauce
¼ tsp each salt and freshly ground black pepper	4 iceberg lettuce leaves, finely sliced
2 tsp vegetable oil	1 large ripe tomato, sliced thinly
	4 large slices tinned beetroot

1   In a large bowl combine all the patty ingredients. Using your hands, work all the ingredients in together. Give them a really good squishing.

2   Using damp hands, form the mince into four large, thin patties. Make sure they are bigger than your hamburger buns as they will shrink when they cook. Place in the fridge for 15 minutes.

3   In a large chef's pan over medium-high heat, place 1 teaspoon oil and cook the patties for 3 minutes each side or until cooked through. Set aside, covered with foil.

4   Heat the remaining oil in the pan and fry the onions until softened and starting to brown. Meanwhile heat the grill. Toast the inside of the buns, then place the tasty cheese on the inside of the top half of the bun and grill until the cheese is starting to melt.

5   To assemble the burgers, spread burger sauce generously over the bottom bun, then add the lettuce, tomato and beetroot. Top with the meat patty, more sauce, and the top of the bun.

Note: Turkish bread or foccacia can be substituted for the burger buns.

Burger sauce

makes 1 cup

Preparation time: 5 minutes

For Paddy's birthday one year, I asked him what he wanted for his birthday dinner. His answer was 'homemade Maccas'. Hmm. So I created this dressing as my version of their special sauce – it's a little bit tangy and gives burgers a bit more of a lift than plain mayo.

½ cup (125 g) whole-egg mayonnaise   1 tbs gherkin relish
1 tbs tomato sauce   ½ brown onion, minced
1 tbs hot English mustard   ¼ tsp salt
2 tsp sugar

Combine all the ingredients in a bowl. Allow the flavours to develop for an hour in the fridge before serving.

'The perfect Sunday? Spending the arvo with my family and friends having a barbecue and a few drinks.' – Tash

'The heart of our home is the garden and pool – it is somewhere beautiful where we all spend time together. We work in the garden as a family and really appreciate how amazing it is to have a backyard like a tropical resort!' – Debbie

Nan at Luna Park in the '50s.

Blackened beef

serves 4

Preparation time: 5 minutes
Cooking time: 10 minutes

The blackness in this beef comes from the butter and also from the high heat on the grill. The mix in this recipe is quite spicy but can be toned down to suit your taste. As with all meat on the barbecue, make sure the steaks have plenty of room on the grill.

2 tsp garlic powder
½ tsp chilli powder
1 tsp dried ground oregano
1 tsp sweet smoked paprika
2 tsp salt

¼ tsp ground black pepper
4 scotch fillet steaks (around 300 g each)
2 tbs butter, melted
a little oil, for brushing grill

1 Preheat a grill plate or barbecue over high heat. Combine the spices and seasonings in a bowl. Brush each steak with butter and press firmly into the spice mix to coat both sides.

2 Brush the grill with a little oil. Cook the steaks for 4 minutes on each side, or until done to your liking. Time will depend on the thickness of the steak. Only turn the steaks once, so they get distinct char lines. Rest the meat for a few minutes before serving. Serve with salad.

'I think the term barbecue is actually a translation of grunts and snorts from the time of the cave man.' – Adam

Sloppy Joe's ribs

serves 4–6, depending how hungry everyone is!

Preparation time: 15 minutes + marinating time
Cooking time: 2 hours

This recipe uses American-style spare ribs. It is one of the all-time favourites in our house – the boys can consume kilos of these. I have called them Sloppy Joe's ribs because they are one of the (admittedly many) dishes that send Joe into his 'food heaven zone', and he usually ends up with sauce from his forehead to his elbows.

1 cup (250 ml) hoisin sauce
⅔ cup (165 ml) rice wine vinegar
½ cup (125 ml) honey
½ cup (125 ml) soy sauce
6 garlic cloves

½ cup (about 120 g) grated fresh ginger
1 tbs Chinese five-spice powder
3 kg pork spare ribs (look for the smaller ones if possible)

1 Combine all ingredients except the ribs with ¼ cup (60 ml) water in a large snap-lock bag. Add the pork ribs and seal the bag well. For best flavour, place it in the fridge overnight (or for at least an hour). Sit the bag in a bowl, and turn the bag occasionally to make sure all the pork is marinated properly.

2 Preheat a covered barbecue to 170°C. Open the bag and transfer the ribs into a baking tray, keeping the marinade aside. Cover the tray with foil and barbecue for 1½ hours. (The best way to roast on a barbecue is to place the baking dish on one half of the barbecue and turn on the elements for the other half. Alternatively, turn on the outside elements and place the baking tray in the middle. This means that heat is circulating without there being direct heat under the dish.)

3 Meanwhile put the reserved marinade into a saucepan (on the side burner of the barbecue if you have one) over medium-high heat and boil until reduced to a syrupy consistency.

4 Remove the foil from the baking tray and brush the marinade generously over the ribs. Return them to the barbecue for a further 30 minutes, uncovered, until the marinade is dark and sticky. Serve with rice and greens, or with potato wedges and salad.

Note: For ribs with a bit of a kick, add ⅓ cup hot chilli sauce to the marinade.

Marinated beef fillet

serves 6

Preparation time: 10 minutes + marinating time
Cooking time: up to 45 minutes

The tender, delicious eye fillet of beef makes a barbecue a gourmet feast.
This is especially great with the balsamic grilled vegetables (page 15).

1 tbs ground fennel	3 garlic cloves, crushed
1 tbs ground coriander seeds	¼ cup (60 g) Dijon mustard
1 tbs ground cumin	1.5 kg eye fillet of beef (thick end)
2 tsp ground red chilli	2 tbs olive oil

1 Combine the spices, garlic and mustard and rub all over the beef fillet. Place into a snap-lock plastic bag and refrigerate for at least 6 hours, or overnight.

2 Preheat the oven or covered barbecue to 180°C (160°C fan-forced). Heat 1 tablespoon olive oil in a large chef's pan over medium-high heat, and brown the meat on all sides. Place the pan into the oven or barbecue. (If you don't have a pan with an oven-proof handle, transfer the meat to a baking tray.)

3 Roast the beef for 20 minutes for rare, 30 minutes for medium or 45 minutes or more for medium to well-done. Rest the beef for at least 10 minutes under foil before carving. Carve and serve with a good quality horseradish cream or hot mustard.

Note: Oven/barbecue temperatures and behaviours will vary. For rare meat, remove the roast when the internal temperature reads 55–57°C. For medium rare, remove at 60–62°C. For medium, remove at 68–70°C. And for well-done, remove at 75°C or above.

For a really fresh spice flavour, use whole seeds instead of pre-ground spices. Toast in a dry frying pan until fragrant and grind in a mortar and pestle.

Roast pumpkin, spinach and ricotta pie

serves 6

Preparation time: 15 minutes
Cooking time: 1 hour 10 minutes

This lovely pie is just right served at room temperature on a picnic. There is no pastry to make – it creates its own delicate crust as it cooks. It can be varied with parmesan grated over the top or some fresh basil stirred through the batter before baking.

½ large butternut pumpkin (about 750 g), peeled and cut into 2 cm dice

⅔ cup (165 ml) light olive oil (or vegetable oil)

½ tsp ground nutmeg

½ tsp salt

¼ tsp ground black pepper

2 brown onions, sliced

2 garlic cloves, chopped

100 g baby spinach

6 eggs

1 cup (150 g) self-raising flour

1 cup (125 g) grated tasty cheese

250 g tub ricotta

1   Preheat oven to 200°C (180°C fan-forced). Grease and flour a 24 cm spring-form cake tin. Toss the pumpkin cubes with 1 tablespoon of the oil, the nutmeg, salt and pepper. Roast in a baking tray for 30 minutes or until soft and golden brown.

2   In a large deep frying pan over medium heat, sauté the onion and garlic in 1 tablespoon oil until soft. Take the pan off the heat and, using tongs, toss the spinach through until wilted slightly.

3   In a bowl beat the eggs. Add the remaining olive oil and mix well. Add flour and whisk until there are no lumps. Stir through the tasty cheese, and season with salt and pepper.

4   Remove the pumpkin from the oven and reduce the temperature to 180°C (160°C fan-forced). Toss the pumpkin through the onion spinach mixture. The spinach will wilt further.

5   Place half the vegetable mixture in the base of the prepared tin and pour half the egg mixture over it. Shake the tin to make sure the egg sinks all around the vegetables. Put the other half of the vegetable mixture on top and pour in the remaining egg mixture.

6   Dollop the ricotta over the top, and, using a spoon, burrow down a little so that there is some ricotta nestled inside the pie as well. Bake for 45 minutes, or until golden brown on top and firm in the middle.

2 Beautiful beginnings

Serving an entrée before a main meal really is the domain of special occasion dinners. Even my most 'domestic goddess-ish' friends don't aim to serve entrées every day of the week.

Although some of the following dishes can be converted into main meals, to me they're a good reason to gather some friends together for a weekend dinner party. As the ancient Greek philosopher Epicurus put so succinctly, 'We should look for someone to eat and drink with rather than looking for something to eat and drink.'

Mick is part of Gosford City Rotary Club, which has a dinner club with a very unusual way of doing things. People are put into groups of four couples, and a dinner party is hosted in each of the four homes every three months – so each couple hosts one dinner party in the year.

The twist is that it's a progressive dinner. I don't mean the exhausting kind where guests have to haul themselves to a different house for each course (which I suspect became less popular all of a sudden when drink-driving laws were introduced). Rather, each couple brings one course for the eight people. So, one couple brings canapés, another brings the entrées, another provides mains and the fourth, dessert. For each dinner party the courses rotate to a different couple, so by the end of the year every couple has had a turn at providing each course. The couple who are doing the mains hosts the event in their home, as it's usually the most work.

There are some huge advantages to this approach. First, it ensures that the group gets together at least every three months – not always an easy feat in a busy life. Second, the effort is shared among all four couples, so it's not such a big expense or amount of work at one time. And third, when you are only focused on one dish, you can give it all of your attention, and as a result some really excellent food is produced.

It's a terrific idea, and I would recommend it to anyone who is keen to spend more time with their friends over a great homemade meal.

Oysters kilpatrick

makes 12

Preparation time: 10 minutes
Cooking time: 5 minutes

At the Narooma oyster festival last year, I was lucky enough to be asked to judge the oyster cooking contest. Each entrant had to create a raw and a cooked oyster dish. There were some wild and wonderful creations, including a few that I maybe won't try at home. I had never eaten so many oysters in one go. I am going back to some old-school favourites with these two – my take on the classics, kilpatrick and mornay.

2 rashers bacon	½ tsp Tabasco
¼ cup (60 ml) tomato sauce	12 fresh oysters
1 tbs Worcestershire sauce	1 tbs flat leaf parsley, finely chopped

1   Preheat the grill to hot. Cut the bacon into the finest strips you can. In a frying pan over high heat, sauté until it goes lightly golden and is starting to crisp.

2   Combine the sauces and Tabasco in a small bowl. Place the oysters on a heatproof tray, on a bed of rock salt so they are stable and level. Divide the bacon among the 12 oysters and top with teaspoonfuls of the sauce.

3   Put under the hot grill for 2 minutes or until the sauce is bubbling. Sprinkle with parsley and serve on a fresh bed of rock salt.

'My worst cooking disaster was the first time I cooked for my boyfriend. I was too busy smiling at him to realise I was about to set the kitchen on fire. We ended up having pizza. We've been married for 15 years now, so fortunately it didn't deter him!' – Rose

Oysters mornay

makes 12

Preparation time: 10 minutes
Cooking time: 10 minutes

20 g butter	½ cup (60 g) grated tasty cheese
1 tbs plain flour	salt and ground white pepper
¾ cup (180 ml) milk	12 fresh oysters
1 tsp Dijon mustard	¼ cup (20 g) freshly grated parmesan cheese

1   Preheat the grill to hot. In a small saucepan over medium heat melt the butter and stir in the flour with a wooden spoon. Keep stirring until the mixture bubbles. Add a splash of milk, stirring all the time. The mixture will come together like a dough. When this happens, add a dash more milk and keep repeating until all the milk is incorporated. If the milk is added too quickly it will form lumps. When all the milk is in the sauce, allow it to boil for a minute or two then add the mustard and tasty cheese. Taste and add salt if necessary, and a pinch of finely ground white pepper.

2   Place the oysters on a heatproof tray, on a bed of rock salt so they are stable and level. Spoon some sauce into each oyster and top with parmesan cheese. Place under the hot grill for 2 minutes or until the cheese is golden and bubbling.

3   Serve on a tray on fresh rock salt. To cut the richness of oyster and cheese, I love to serve some fresh lemon wedges on the side.

*'One of my favourite memories is sitting up on
the kitchen bench while my wonderful Mum was cooking.
We would chat about my day at school.' – Tash*

My little sister Debbie, with her big catch.

Vietnamese chicken soup

serves 6

Preparation time: 15 minutes
Cooking time: 10 minutes

On a cook's tour of Vietnam recently, our first meal was at a funny little pho restaurant with laminated tables, plastic chairs and bright lights. I ordered a chicken pho, or clear broth soup, and it was incredible. The flavour in the crystal-clear broth was rich and the vegetables were the freshest I think I have ever eaten. This is my simplification of an awesome travel memory.

2 skinless chicken breasts, fat removed
8 cups (2 litres) chicken stock
2 cm piece ginger, sliced
2 garlic cloves, halved
1 large green chilli, deseeded
4 shallots

1 bunch Asian greens (such as choy sum or bok choy), shredded finely
1 bunch coriander
½ bunch mint, leaves picked
1 cup (80 g) bean sprouts

1   Place the chicken breasts into a large pot and cover with the stock. Place over medium-low heat and while it is coming up to a simmer, add the ginger, garlic, half the chilli cut into 3 pieces, the white parts of 2 shallots and the washed stems and roots of the coriander.

2   Simmer for 15 minutes or until the chicken is cooked through. Remove the chicken and slice very finely, or shred. Simmer the soup for another few minutes then strain into a clean pot.

3   Meanwhile, into four deep noodle bowls, divide the greens and top with the remaining 2 shallots (very finely sliced), a few coriander leaves, a few mint leaves, and the shredded chicken.

4   Make sure the broth is very hot, and pour it into the bowls. Top with bean sprouts and a few very fine slices of the remaining chilli.

'The three of us boys have jobs every night. Whoever helps Mum cook gets out of the washing up so we all like to cook. We all help because in a family everyone has to do their bit.' – Tom

Spiced pumpkin and coconut soup

serves 4

Preparation time: 10 minutes
Cooking time: 25 minutes

I love food that makes life easy. This soup can be made a day or two before you want to eat it, and simply reheated. As with many spiced dishes the flavours actually improve over a few days.

1 tbs vegetable oil	750 g pumpkin, peeled, deseeded
1 brown onion, chopped	and roughly chopped
4 garlic cloves, crushed	2 cups (500 ml) salt-reduced chicken stock
2.5 cm piece ginger, peeled and finely chopped	(or vegetable for a vegetarian dish)
2 red chillies, deseeded and finely chopped	2 x 400 ml tins coconut ~~cream~~ MILK.
1 tsp ground coriander	salt and freshly ground black pepper
1 tsp ground cumin	½ cup (125 g) plain yoghurt
½ tsp ground cardamom	coriander leaves (optional)
½ tsp ground cinnamon	OPTIONAL PRAWNS + CRAB WARMED THOUG
	ADDED WHEN READY TO SEVER.

1   Heat the oil in a large, heavy-based saucepan with a lid. Add the onion, garlic, ginger, chillies and spices. Cook, stirring constantly, until the onion is soft and the spices fragrant, about 10 minutes.

2   Add the pumpkin, stock and coconut cream and bring to the boil. Put the lid on the saucepan and simmer for 15 minutes, stirring occasionally. Using a hand-held blender, blend the soup until smooth. Season with salt and pepper.

3   Ladle into serving bowls, and top each portion with a dollop of yoghurt. Garnish with coriander (if using).

'I have never delivered meals to friends and family.
This is mainly in consideration for their own health and safety.' – Tony

Hearty pea and ham soup

makes about 3 litres

Preparation time: 15 minutes
Cooking time: 3 hours

My mum used to make this soup in her big orange and brown '70s crockpot.
The smell of it in the house reminds me of those childhood days when it was cold and
grey outside, and we were so glad to be in the warmth and light of the kitchen.

1 tbs olive oil
1 brown onion, roughly chopped
1 garlic clove, chopped
1 carrot, diced

1.2 kg ham hocks (see Note)
500 g green split peas
2 cups (300 g) frozen peas

1 Heat the oil in a very large pot over medium-high heat. Sauté the onion, garlic and carrot for
2 minutes or until starting to soften. Add the hocks and cover with 2 litres water. Add the split
peas to the pot.

2 Reduce the heat to low and simmer gently, covered, for around 2½ hours. You may need to top the
water up to keep the ham hocks covered, but try not to add any more than necessary or it will just
need to be reduced at the end. The split peas should be completely soft. Remove the ham hocks and
set aside to cool.

3 Add the frozen peas to the pot and turn the heat off after 1 minute. The frozen peas give a brighter
green colour and fresh flavour. Using a hand-held blender, blitz the soup in the pot until all the
ingredients are completely pureed and velvet smooth. If you don't have a stick mixer, transfer the
soup in batches to a blender.

4 If the soup is too thin for your liking, simmer for a bit longer until it reduces and thickens. Remove
the skin, bone and fatty bits from the hocks. Shred or slice the meat – the consistency is up to you.
I like it quite fine so each mouthful of soup has some pieces of ham in it – others like bigger chunks
of meat. Return the ham to the soup and serve with a grind of black pepper, and a robust bread such
as toasted sourdough or warm crusty rolls.

Note: Instead of ham hocks you can use a similar amount of bacon bones. I prefer the hock as you
get more meat from it and there's less chance you'll get fiddly little bones in the soup.

The soup solidifies as it goes cold, but will thin out again on reheating. For minted pea and ham
soup, add ½ cup firmly packed mint leaves with the frozen peas.

Roast tomato and goats' cheese tarts

serves 4

Preparation time: 10 minutes
Cooking time: 20 minutes

These are an easy-to-make vegetarian entrée. They are lovely piping hot but just as nice at room temperature. You can also make one long oblong tart and cut it into slices.

4 sheets frozen puff pastry	4 eggs
16 cherry tomatoes, halved	1 tbs cream
1 tbs olive oil	2 tbs fresh thyme leaves, chopped
2 tbs balsamic vinegar	1 cup (125 g) grated tasty cheese
salt and pepper	180 g goats' cheese

1   Preheat oven to 200°C (180°C fan-forced). Line four 15 cm individual tart pans with partially thawed puff pastry. Trim pastry around the edges and prick well with a fork. Line with non-stick baking paper and fill with rice or pastry weights. Bake for 10 minutes or until a pale golden colour. Remove from the oven and take out the paper and weights.

2   Place halved tomatoes, cut side up, on a lined baking tray and drizzle with olive oil and balsamic vinegar. Season with salt and pepper. Roast for 10 minutes or until starting to wilt.

3   Beat the eggs with the cream, thyme and a pinch of salt and pepper. Sprinkle the tasty cheese evenly into the pastry cases. Place 8 tomato halves neatly in each pastry case, cut side up. Sprinkle goats' cheese around the tomatoes.

4   Gently pour the egg mixture into the tart cases and bake for 10–12 minutes or until the egg has set and the top is golden. Serve sprinkled with some additional balsamic vinegar.

Note: I serve this as an entrée, but it would make a lovely light meal accompanied by a salad or steamed vegetables.

Crispy king prawns

serves 4

Preparation time: 10 minutes
Cooking time: 15 minutes

What can I tell you – I love prawns. Sizzling in garlic oil, on the barbecue,
on top of a steak with creamy sauce, or cooked whole and peeled fresh ... I just love them.
These can be served with smoked paprika aioli (overleaf), sweet chilli
or soy ginger dipping sauce.

vegetable oil, for deep frying
¼ cup (35 g) cornflour
¼ tsp garlic powder
¼ tsp salt
¼ tsp ground white pepper
¾ cup (115 g) self-raising flour
1 egg, lightly beaten
750 g raw green king prawns, peeled, tails intact

2 Lebanese cucumbers, halved and seeded,
   very finely sliced diagonally
½ fennel bulb,
   very finely shredded (chiffonnade)
2 shallots, very finely sliced lengthways
2 tbs sugar
2 tbs white wine vinegar
⅓ cup (80 ml) olive oil

1   Fill a deep-fryer to the recommended level with vegetable oil and heat to 190°C. Alternatively, half-fill a medium saucepan with vegetable oil and use a kitchen thermometer for temperature.

2   Combine the cornflour, garlic powder, salt and pepper in a bowl. In a second bowl, combine the flour, egg and 1½ cups (375 ml) of iced water to create a thin batter.

3   Toss about eight prawns into the cornflour mixture, and shake off the excess. Using tongs, dip each one into the batter, then drop into the hot oil. Don't cook more than eight at a time or the temperature of the oil will drop and the prawns will take too long to cook, making them tough. If using a deep-fryer, make sure the basket is lowered into the oil first, or the prawns will stick to it. When prawns are a light golden brown, remove them to drain on paper towels.

4   Toss the cucumber, fennel and shallots together. Combine the sugar, vinegar and oil in a jug. Just before serving pour the dressing over the salad and mix well.

5   Serve the prawns on a plate alongside the cucumber and fennel salad, with lemon cheeks and aioli (see overleaf).

Smoked paprika aioli

makes about 1 cup

Preparation time: 10 minutes

As well as being an accompaniment for the prawns, this is great
on a chicken burger or instead of mayonnaise on sandwiches.

3 egg yolks
1 garlic clove, crushed
1 tbs lemon juice
⅓ cup (80 ml) olive oil

½ cup (125 ml) vegetable oil
(such as canola or sunflower)
1 tsp smoked paprika

1   Place the egg yolks, garlic, lemon juice and a pinch of salt into a small bowl and whisk until smooth.
    Use either a hand-held whisk, an electric hand beater or an electric mixer – whatever is easiest for
    you.

2   Combine the oils in a jug and pour into the egg yolk mixture, drop by drop, making sure to whisk
    continuously. As the mixture thickens, you can add the oil a little faster – in a slow steady stream
    rather than drops.

3   Continue until all the oil has been incorporated and the aioli is thick. Add the paprika, then taste
    and adjust the seasoning. Cover and refrigerate.

*'I used to watch my Dad throwing stuff around the kitchen,
making out he didn't know what he was doing – and then having
a really nice meal and thinking he must have fluked it.' – Kieron*

*'One of the best times I remember was having a
Sunday roast. Dad was throwing peas in Great-Nan's
hair and Great-Nan was throwing them back!'* – Luke

My sister Debbie's kids ... 'When we grow up, these will be our rules':
'Everyone eats together once a day.' – Sam
'No feet on the dinner table.' – Luke
'You eat what you're given even if you don't like it.' – Lauren
'You don't have to eat anything you don't like.' – Jess

My boys ... 'When we grow up, these will be our table rules':
'Taste your food before you put salt on it.' – Mick
'No burping at the table ... or if you do, say "excuse me".' – Joe
'You have to at least wear pants to the table.' – Tom
'You must bless the cook (which will be me).' – Paddy

Debbie and her boy Luke, and me
with Joe – and Tom on the way!

Pea risotto with scallops and chorizo

serves 4 as an entrée

Preparation time: 20 minutes
Cooking time: 50 minutes

This is an elegant dinner party dish. Risotto isn't as tricky as it's made out to be,
just as long as the rice is cooked (which you can easily test by tasting it), but not
cooked until it's mush. The secret of lovely seared scallops is to pat them dry,
use a nice hot pan, and leave them plenty of room so they don't stew.

1½ cups (225 g) frozen baby peas	¾ cup (165 g) arborio rice
50 g butter	⅓ cup (80 ml) dry white wine
salt and pepper	½ cup (40 g) freshly grated parmesan
4 cups (1 litre) chicken stock	1 chorizo sausage
2 tbs olive oil	1 tbs olive oil
1 small brown onion, finely chopped	12 scallops, without roe
1 garlic clove, crushed	extra virgin olive oil, to serve

1   Cook the peas to packet directions – either in a small pot of boiling water, or in the microwave.
Keep aside 2 tablespoons of peas for serving. Place the rest of the peas into a food processor with
half the butter and process until smooth. Taste, and season with salt and pepper.

2   Bring the stock to a simmer in a medium saucepan and keep it simmering while the risotto is being
made. Heat half the oil and the remaining butter together in a medium pan and cook the onion and
garlic for 3–4 minutes or until softened and translucent. Add rice and continue to stir for a further
minute until the grains start to become translucent.

3   Add the wine and allow rice to fully absorb the liquid. Add the hot stock a ladleful at a time, allowing
each to be absorbed before adding the next. Continue, stirring gently for 15–20 minutes or until rice
is tender but still has a bite (al dente). You may not need all the stock – the result you are looking
for is grains that are still formed, not broken or mushy, but with no hard or chalky bit in the middle.
Stir in pea puree and parmesan. Taste again and season if required, bearing in mind that parmesan
can be very salty.

Continued next page ...

Pea risotto with scallops and chorizo *continued ...*

4 Peel the chorizo and cut into little batons about 3 cm long and 5 mm in thickness. Fry the batons in a frying pan over medium-high heat, until crispy. Drain on paper towel and keep any oil in the pan.

5 Heat the remaining oil in the pan over medium-high heat. Season scallops with a little salt and cook for 1–2 minutes on the first side, until the scallop develops a lovely brown crust. Turn over and cook for another 30–60 seconds until still tender in the centre.

6 To serve, place a generous spoonful of risotto in warmed bowls. Top with three scallops and scatter with chorizo batons and reserved baby peas. Drizzle with extra virgin olive oil, and serve immediately.

'I have "Mum cooking" and "fun cooking". Mum cooking is whacking out a meal at 6 pm, five nights a week, mainly old favourites and easy meals. Fun cooking is going through my books and magazines, shopping specially for the ingredients and taking my time. It's more experimental, fancier ingredients, more complex recipes.' – Steph

Our family has a history of camping and caravanning that spans generations. When I was 11, we loaded up the van and spent three months travelling around Australia. We went down mines and up mountains, snorkelled reefs and crossed deserts, even had the van overturn and had to rebuild it in the middle of the Outback. I owe much of my appreciation for this amazing country to that trip and others we took. The old van that my grandfather built has been kept in immaculate condition and is still registered and roadworthy today.

Chicken and leek terrine

serves 6 as an entrée

Preparation time: 20 minutes
Cooking time: 1 hour

This is a great do-ahead dish for a dinner party. It can be made one or two days
in advance, then just sliced and served on the night. It is great for a posh picnic too.

500 g chicken thigh fillets
1 chicken breast fillet (about 250 g)
½ cup (80 g) pine nuts
20 g butter
1 leek, white and pale green parts, finely sliced
2 garlic cloves, crushed

1 tbs fresh thyme leaves
½ tsp salt
¼ tsp ground white pepper
1 egg, lightly beaten
10–12 slices prosciutto

1 Preheat the oven to 180°C (160°C fan-forced). Mince half of the chicken thigh fillets in a food
   processor, and cut the other half into 2 cm pieces. Cut the breast fillet into 2 cm pieces. Combine
   in a large mixing bowl.

2 Place the pine nuts into a medium frying pan over medium-low heat, and shake gently until they
   are starting to brown. Watch them carefully as once they start to brown they can burn very quickly.
   Remove from the pan and set aside to cool.

3 Return the pan to the heat and place in it the butter, leek, garlic and thyme. Sauté gently
   for 5 minutes or until the leek is soft and fragrant. Remove from the heat and allow to cool.

4 When the leek mixture is cool, add it to the chicken, along with the pine nuts, salt and pepper.
   Knead the mixture vigorously with your hands until well combined. Add the egg and mix through.

5 Line a medium loaf tin with foil, leaving some to overhang the sides. Lay the prosciutto into the
   tin. Make sure that the pieces overlap in the base, and also that there is plenty of overhang. Leave
   no gaps. Fill the lined tin with the chicken mixture and press it in. Cover with foil and seal tightly.
   Bake for 1 hour, until firm to the touch.

6 Place the loaf tin on the sink or on a tea towel. Place a second loaf tin on top and press down to
   release excess juice. Put a couple of tins into the top loaf tin (tinned tomatoes for example) to weigh
   it down, and refrigerate overnight.

7 To unmould, take the foil off the top and turn the tin upside down. There will be some jelly-like
   aspic on the outside of the terrine, which can be wiped off with a paper towel. Cut into slices and
   serve with sweet chilli and ginger jam (see overleaf), or any sweet fruit relish.

Sweet chilli and ginger jam

makes 1⅓ cups

Preparation time: 20 minutes
Cooking time: 1½ hours

There are a number of ways in which I take after my nan. One of them is a love of
condiments. Just like Nan's used to, my fridge has a couple of shelves devoted to jams,
chutneys, mustards, mayos, sauces and pastes. This sweet and savoury jam is great not just
as a condiment but also as an ingredient to give a lift to stir-fries and casseroles too.

2 red capsicums
10 long red chillies, deseeded and coarsely chopped
6 garlic cloves, chopped
10 cm piece ginger, peeled and chopped

¾ cup (150 g) light brown sugar
⅓ cup (80 ml) white vinegar
2 tbs fish sauce

1 Cut the capsicums into large flat pieces, and place skin side up under a hot grill until the skin is
   black and blistered. Transfer to a plastic bag for about 10 minutes, then slip off the skins. Coarsely
   chop the flesh.

2 Place capsicum, chillies, garlic and ginger into the bowl of a food processor and add 1 tablespoon of
   water. Process until broken down and smooth.

3 Pour the mixture into a large saucepan and stir in sugar and vinegar. Bring to the boil, then reduce
   the heat to low and simmer for 1 hour, stirring occasionally. As the jam cooks, skim off any foamy
   scum that rises to the surface. Add fish sauce and continue to cook for a further 30 minutes.

4 As the jam thickens, stir continuously to prevent it from sticking. The jam is ready when the spoon
   you are using starts to leave a trail and the bottom of the pan can be seen briefly. Turn off the heat
   and pour into sterilised jars.

Salt and pepper squid

serves 4

Preparation time: 10 minutes
Cooking time: 10 minutes

The key to tender squid is to cook it quickly so that it doesn't end up tough.
It needs to be served immediately after cooking.

4 squid tubes, cleaned
vegetable oil, for deep frying
½ cup (70 g) cornflour
1 tsp salt
½ tsp ground white pepper

½ tsp cracked black pepper
½ tsp garlic powder
½ tsp ground dried chillies
½ tsp Chinese five-spice

1 Cut the squid tubes open and lay flat. Using the blade of a knife, gently scrape the very fine membrane covering the squid to rough it up a bit. Score the squid in a criss-cross pattern and cut into strips about 2 cm wide.

2 Fill a deep-fryer to the recommended level with clean vegetable oil and heat it to 200°C. Alternatively, half-fill a large pan and use a kitchen thermometer for temperature.

3 Combine the cornflour and spices in a bowl. Toss the squid through, coating thoroughly.

4 Fry the squid in small batches to maintain the heat in the oil. Each batch should take 1–1½ minutes to turn a light golden brown. Serve with lemon wedges, tartare or sweet chilli sauce, and green salad.

'The kitchen is the heart of our home – there is so much there that warms our souls, be it a cup of tea, a slice of toast, a shared meal.' – Pauline

Beautiful beginnings

Seafood crêpes

serves 4

Preparation time: 15 minutes
Cooking time: 20 minutes

These are delicately flavoured, elegant starters for a nice dinner party.
These quantities would also serve two people as a main course.

Crêpes
½ cup (75 g) plain flour
2 eggs, lightly beaten
¾ cup (180 ml) milk
cold butter, to grease

Filling
½ cup (125 ml) dry white wine
180 g Atlantic salmon fillet, skin off
8 green king prawns, shelled and deveined,
cut in half

4 sea scallops, without roe
20 g butter
1 tbs plain flour
⅔ cup (160 ml) milk
2 tbs Dijon mustard
¼ tsp salt
¼ tsp ground white pepper
⅓ cup (80 ml) cream
2 shallots, white and pale green parts, sliced
¼ cup flat leaf parsley

1 bunch baby asparagus

1   To make the crêpes, place the flour into a bowl and add the eggs and milk. Whisk well to ensure there are no lumps.

2   Rub a stick of butter over the base of a crêpe pan or non-stick frying pan. Pour ¼ cup (60 ml) batter into the base of the pan and quickly swirl to make a thin circle. Cook for 1 minute, then flip and cook for a further 30 seconds. The crêpe should be golden brown. Repeat with the butter and batter until all is used. You should make about six crêpes – you will only need four, but this allows for a couple of practice ones. You may need to turn the temperature down slightly during cooking time, as the pan gets hotter the longer you go. Put the crêpes on a plate and cover with a clean tea towel to keep warm.

Continued overleaf ...

Seafood crêpes *continued ...*

3   For the filling, wipe out the pan and heat the wine over medium heat. When the wine is simmering very gently, place the salmon in the pan. Poach for 2 minutes on each side, then add the prawns and scallops. Bring back to the simmer and poach for a further couple of minutes. Using a slotted spoon, remove the seafood from the wine. Take the pan off the heat for a couple of minutes until the wine cools slightly.

4   Add the butter and flour to the pan with the wine, stirring constantly. Add the milk just a dribble at a time. The milk will incorporate into the flour and make a dough. Once it comes together, add a little more milk at a time, stirring until smooth between each addition, until it is all incorporated. Add the mustard, then taste and add salt and pepper. Stir through the cream. Once the sauce has heated through, turn the heat off.

5   Stir through the shallots, then break up the salmon into chunks and gently stir it through the sauce along with the other seafood and the parsley.

6   Blanch or microwave the baby asparagus for 1–2 minutes, or until tender but still with a bit of bite. Dot with butter and cover with foil to keep warm.

7   Put a crêpe onto a plate and place one scallop, four prawn halves, and about a quarter of the salmon into the centre, along with some of the sauce. Carefully fold over the sides and ends of the crêpe and the ends, to make a neat rectangle. Gently flip the crêpe so the joins are at the bottom, onto a bed of baby asparagus. Serve with a cheek of lemon.

'Mum used to make great hearty meals. She always seemed to enjoy looking after everyone and making sure no one was hungry. Even if we said, "No, thank you," there would be more served up.' – Kelly

'We were on holidays in Queensland and we were having breakfast outside. Two lorikeets hopped onto our table. One started to eat my blueberry muffin and the other one stuck its head in my orange juice and started drinking it. Then a cockatoo swooped inside the restaurant and came flying back out with a whole piece of toast in its beak!' – Paddy

3 | The main event

Early in our marriage, before we had kids, we arranged for some good friends to come over for dinner. I roasted a chicken – it was stuffed, and trussed, and massaged with butter, and basted until it was crispy and golden. It was beautiful.

Just before the guests arrived I took it from the oven and placed it lovingly in the centre of the table along with all the side dishes I had prepared, and ducked into my room to freshen up. I came back into the dining room to a sight so shocking that I froze to the spot for a second. Our beautiful, big, jet-black cattle dog Charlie was standing on the table – *on the table* – with the whole chicken in his mouth. Not just a piece of it – he had managed to get a good enough grip to pick up the whole thing.

When I got over my shock I gave chase, but he wasn't giving this bounty up easily. It ended badly for the dog, and even worse for the chicken. By the time I prised it from Charlie's jaws my beautiful roasted bird was a shredded collection of cracked bones and drool.

Right about then the doorbell rang. To this day I can't remember what I did instead of chicken – probably a mercy dash to the supermarket for something quick and easy. What I do remember is having a great old laugh about it afterwards.

Dinner doesn't always have to be a roaring culinary success. Sometimes it's enough to gather together, to have a laugh, to share the day, to create some memories. Sometimes it's enough to have tried something new in a spirit of adventure, and swear to do better next time. As my brother-in-law Anthony says, it's all about the intent of the cook.

My intent on that night long ago was to lovingly prepare a meal to share with friends. And I did – we just didn't get to eat it. The chicken may not have made it, but the evening was a success anyway – good intentions, good friends and laughter saved the day.

Chinese-style braised pork rashers

serves 4

Preparation time: 5 minutes
Cooking time: 1 hour 10 minutes

Don't be put off by the long cooking time for this dish – mostly the pork is just happily bubbling away with no input required. The end result is worth it – tender pork in deliciously rich gravy.

1.5 kg pork rashers (pork belly strips)
1 tsp Chinese five-spice
5 cm piece ginger, peeled and finely sliced
10–12 garlic cloves, crushed
¼ cup (60 ml) soy sauce

¼ cup (60 ml) oyster sauce
½ cup (100 g) brown sugar
½ tsp chilli powder
2 tbs cornflour

1   In a large pot over medium-high heat place the pork belly with 3 cups (750 ml) water. Add the Chinese five-spice, ginger, garlic, soy sauce, oyster sauce, brown sugar and chilli powder. Stir together and bring to the boil.

2   Reduce the heat to low and simmer uncovered for an hour, or until the pork skin is gelatinous and the meat tender.

3   Remove the pork from the pot and increase the heat to high. Cook for about 5 minutes at a rapid boil until the sauce has reduced by half.

4   Dissolve the cornflour in ¼ cup (60 ml) water, and stir into the sauce. Simmer for another couple of minutes until the cornflour is cooked and the sauce has thickened. Serve the rashers smothered in sauce, with steamed rice and Asian greens.

'When I was a teenager I would sometimes walk to Grandma's from school for a hot lunch. I was treated to a full roast dinner followed by waffles fresh off the iron with whipped cream. The other boys at school were very jealous!' – Saul

Balsamic lamb rump

serves 4

Preparation time: 5 minutes
Cooking time: 20 minutes

Tender lamb rump only needs to be marinated for a fairly short time, as it takes flavours on board well. The marinade is then cooked as the sauce in this simple dish.

¼ cup (60 ml) good quality balsamic vinegar
2 garlic cloves, crushed
4 lamb rumps (250–300 g each)

1 tbs olive oil
salt and pepper
2 tbs brown sugar

1 Preheat the oven to 200°C (180°C fan-forced). Combine the balsamic vinegar and garlic in a Pyrex (or any non-metallic) dish, and add the lamb. Turn it to coat, and leave to marinate for 15 minutes. Remove the lamb from the marinade, reserving marinade.

2 Heat the olive oil in a non-stick frying pan over medium-high heat. Season the lamb with salt and pepper, and pan fry for 2–4 minutes on all sides or until cooked to your liking. The time will depend on the size of the rumps. Remove from pan and rest the meat, covered with foil.

3 Pour the marinade into the pan with ¼ cup (60 ml) water and the brown sugar. Bring to the boil and simmer for a few minutes until the sauce thickens slightly. Taste, and season with salt and pepper. Great with smashed potatoes (page 114) and greens.

'I love cooking – it's my favourite leisure activity.
Usually with a glass of wine and music playing.' – Francine

Lamb korma

serves 4–6

Preparation time: 20 minutes + marinating time
Cooking time: about 1 hour 45 minutes

I have always enjoyed Indian food, but the opportunity to travel to India and eat it in the humidity and chaos and colour of that beautiful country gave me a whole new appreciation – not only of Indian cuisine and culture, but also of our own beautiful land and the food that we can access.

1 tbs ground coriander	3 garlic cloves, chopped
2 tsp ground cumin	½ cup (60 g) ground almonds
1 tsp ground cardamom	2 tbs vegetable oil
1 tsp ground turmeric	5 whole cloves
⅓ cup (80 g) natural Greek yoghurt	1 cinnamon stick
1.2 kg lamb leg, cut into 2.5 cm cubes	1 teaspoon salt
2 large red onions, peeled	400 ml tin coconut cream
5 cm piece ginger, peeled and chopped	

1   Stir the ground spices into the yoghurt in a large bowl. Stir the lamb through it thoroughly. Marinate for at least half an hour.

2   Coarsely chop one of the onions and place into a blender or food processor with the ginger, garlic and ground almonds. Process until a smooth paste forms (you may need to add a little water to bring the mixture together).

3   Heat the oil in a large enamelled cast-iron casserole dish over medium-low heat. Thickly slice the remaining onion and cook for 10 minutes, stirring occasionally, until the onion is a deep golden brown and completely softened. Add the paste and continue cooking for a further 2–3 minutes, or until fragrant and the paste has dried out a little.

4   Add the lamb mixture, whole spices, salt, coconut cream and ¾ cup (180 ml) water and mix well. Cover and bring to a simmer. Cook for 1 hour, stirring occasionally. Remove the lid and continue to cook for a further 30–40 minutes or until the curry has thickened and the meat is tender. Taste, and season with extra salt if required. Serve with steamed basmati rice.

Note: If you don't have a flameproof enamelled casserole dish use any large heavy-based pan. You can get your butcher to bone the lamb leg for you if you like.

The main event

Tomato kasundi

makes 4 cups

Preparation time: 30 minutes
Cooking time: 1½ hours

One of our first meals in India was in a traditional southern Indian restaurant. Food was served on a banana leaf and we ate with our hands. Condiments are central to the Indian dining experience, and are traditionally scooped up with some rice or flatbread, and whatever curry is being served.

6 cm piece fresh ginger, peeled and chopped

4 large garlic cloves, peeled and chopped

2 long green chillies, deseeded and coarsely chopped

⅓ cup (80 ml) vegetable oil

1 tbs black mustard seeds

leaves stripped from 2 stems curry leaves

1 large onion, peeled and coarsely chopped

2 tbs ground cumin

1 tbs ground turmeric

1 tbs paprika

1 tbs dry mustard powder

½ cup (125 ml) brown malt vinegar

1.5 kg ripe tomatoes, washed and roughly chopped

¾ cup (165 g) white sugar

1 tbs salt

1   Place the ginger, garlic and chopped chilli into a mortar and pound with a pestle until broken down to a thick paste. Alternatively, place into a food processor and process until smooth.

2   Heat the oil in a large saucepan over medium heat and add the mustard seeds. Fry for 1 minute or until they begin to pop and crackle. Stir in the curry leaves and cook a further minute. Add the chopped onion, stirring for 1 minute until it starts to soften. Add the paste and continue cooking until the onion has softened and the mixture is fragrant.

3   Stir in the dry spices and mustard powder, and cook for a further 1–2 minutes, making sure not to burn the spices. Add the remaining ingredients and mix well.

4   Bring to the boil. Reduce the heat to low and simmer, stirring occasionally, for 1½ hours or until thick and jammy. Spoon into sterilised jars and seal tightly. Cool, label and date the jars.

Note: If fresh curry leaves are not available, use dry ones from the herb and spice rack of your supermarket. Keep the chutney in a cool dark place – the flavour improves with time, so if you can, store for about 1 month before using. Once opened, it will keep in the fridge for up to 6 weeks.

Filet mignon with mushrooms

serves 4

Preparation time: 15 minutes
Cooking time: 20 minutes

When I was a kid our family didn't eat out at restaurants very often, saving our money instead for camping trips. So when I was invited to my best friend's birthday dinner at the Black Stump, it was a real treat. I still remember ordering the New York cut, and thinking it was the best thing I had ever eaten. Filet mignon is a classic. It reminds me of the good old days when, for me at least, the Black Stump was the pinnacle of dining experiences.

4 rindless bacon rashers	300 g button mushrooms, sliced
4 thick eye-fillet steaks, about 300 g each	¼ cup (60 ml) brandy
1 tbs vegetable oil	¼ cup (60 ml) cream
20 g butter	

1   Preheat oven to 200°C (180°C fan-forced). Trim the bacon to the thickness of the steak, and wrap a rasher around the edge of each fillet, securing with toothpicks. Heat the oil in a large non-stick frypan with an ovenproof handle. Season the steaks with salt and pepper and sear over high heat on all sides (including the bacon). This should take 3–4 minutes.

2   Place the pan containing the steaks in the oven for around 15 minutes depending on the way you like it cooked.

3   Meanwhile, melt the butter in a frying pan and sauté the mushrooms over medium-high heat until soft. Season with salt and pepper.

4   Remove the pan from the oven, being very careful with the hot handle! Take the steaks out of the pan and remove the toothpicks. Set aside under foil to rest. Place the pan over medium heat and pour the brandy in. Flambé if you like (see Note), or just cook for a couple of minutes until reduced and the raw alcohol smell is gone. Pour in the cream and toss the mushrooms. Serve on top of the steak, alongside some roasted chat potatoes and steamed asparagus.

Note: You can sear the meat several hours in advance, then finish in the oven just before serving. Be sure to remove the meat from the fridge well beforehand to allow it to come back to room temperature before placing it in the oven.

To flambé the brandy, tilt the pan slightly (assuming you have a gas cooker) and the fumes will catch alight. Be careful!

Chicken with almonds

Serves 4–6

Preparation time: 10 minutes
Cooking time: 10 minutes

My sister-in-law, Andrea, was raised in Canada by a Chinese father and
Trinidadian mother, which has made for some fantastically diverse meals
and traditions in her family. This is one of her family recipes.

1 kg chicken breast fillets, cut into 2 cm dice
2 tbs Shaoxing cooking wine or dry sherry
2 tbs light soy sauce
1 tbs sugar
2 carrots, peeled and cut into 1 cm dice
2 tbs peanut or vegetable oil
110 g whole blanched almonds

3 celery sticks, cut into 1 cm dice
227 g can sliced water chestnuts, drained
225 g can bamboo shoots, drained
2 tbs cornflour
1 cup (250 ml) chicken stock
salt and ground white pepper

1   Combine the chicken, wine, soy sauce and sugar in a large bowl and mix well. Set aside to marinate
    while preparing remaining ingredients.

2   Cook the carrots in the microwave on High (or blanch in boiling water) for 2 minutes. Heat 2
    teaspoons of the oil in a large wok over high heat. Add the almonds and cook for 1–2 minutes, or
    until just golden. Remove and set aside.

3   Add one third of the remaining oil to the hot wok. Cook one third of the chicken until browned
    and sealed but not cooked through; set aside. Repeat twice more with remaining oil and chicken.
    Add the cooked carrots and the celery and stir-fry for 2 minutes. Toss through the water chestnuts
    and bamboo shoots, and return the chicken to the wok.

4   Dissolve the cornflour in the chicken stock and pour over the chicken and vegetables. Simmer for
    5 minutes, or until the chicken is cooked through and sauce is thick and glossy. Taste, and season
    with salt and pepper. Scatter the toasted almonds over the top and serve with steamed rice.

Moussaka

serves 8 as a main, 12–16 as part of a buffet

Preparation time: 30 minutes
Cooking time: 1 hour

This is a great dish to take to a party or to feed a large number of people as part of a buffet. It can also be done in advance as it reheats beautifully.

4–5 large eggplants, cut into 1 cm slices
vegetable oil, for frying
1 kg lamb or beef mince
2 onions, finely diced
3 garlic cloves, chopped
2 tsp ground cinnamon
½ tsp ground allspice

2 tbs tomato paste
1 cup (250 ml) tomato purée or passata
½ cup (125 ml) red wine
125 g butter
½ cup (75 g) plain flour
3 cups (750 ml) milk
1½ cups (120 g) grated parmesan

1   Preheat the oven to 180°C (160°C fan forced). Salt the eggplant slices on both sides and place them between 2 layers of paper towel for around 15 minutes. Wipe carefully with a fresh paper towel to remove salt and liquid.

2   Heat ½ cm oil in a large frying pan and cook the eggplant in batches over medium-high heat until browned. Top up the oil as needed.

3   Brown the mince in the same pan. Add the onion and garlic and cook for a further minute. Add the cinnamon and allspice and cook for another minute. Add the tomato paste and stir to combine then stir in the tomato purée and red wine. Cook until the liquid has evaporated and the mixture is quite dry.

4   For the béchamel sauce, heat a medium saucepan over medium-low heat and add the butter and flour. Cook, stirring, for 2–3 minutes. Add a splash of milk. The mixture will straightaway form a dough. Keep stirring and adding milk a little at a time. When all the milk is added, stir (using a wire whisk if there are any lumps) and allow the sauce to thicken and the flour to fully cook. Stir in 1 cup (80 g) of the parmesan. Taste, and add salt if required. Remove from heat.

5   To assemble, place a layer of eggplant slices in the base of a 24 x 36 cm baking dish. Top with half the meat mixture. Repeat. Finish with a layer of eggplant slices and cover with the béchamel sauce. Sprinkle the remaining cheese over the top and bake for 30 minutes or until golden brown on top.

Monterey chicken

serves 4

Preparation time: 15 minutes
Cooking time: 15 minutes

Chicken, bacon and cheese are a winning combination at our place,
so this dish is a favourite – moist chicken breast topped with bacon,
sweet barbecue flavours and bubbling golden mozzarella.

4 small skinless chicken breast fillets

1 tbs olive oil

3 bacon rashers, finely chopped

200 g button mushrooms, halved if large, finely sliced

⅓ cup (80 ml) barbecue sauce

2 tbs tomato paste

1 tbs Worcestershire sauce

1 cup (100 g) grated mozzarella cheese

1 Carefully slice each chicken breast fillet horizontally, so that it is in two evenly-sized pieces. Gently pound with a meat mallet so that the fillets are an even thickness.

2 Heat oil in a large non-stick frypan over medium-high heat. Pan-fry the chicken, a few pieces at a time, for around 2 minutes on each side, or until golden brown and just cooked through. Be wary of over-cooking or it will be very dry. Remove the chicken from the pan and keep warm under foil.

3 In the same pan, sauté the bacon until starting to brown, then add the mushrooms. Sauté until the mushrooms are soft and cooked.

4 Add the barbecue sauce, tomato paste and Worcestershire sauce and cook for a further minute. Place the chicken on a foil-lined baking tray. Put a spoonful of the bacon mixture onto each piece and carefully press it all over the top. Sprinkle mozzarella on top. Cook under a hot grill for 2–3 minutes, or until golden and bubbling. Delicious served with salad and corn fritters.

'Our family dinners are the heart of our home, they bring us together. Most of the time it is the only chance we get to sit together and discuss our lives.' – Brie

Creamy bacon fettuccine

serves 4

Preparation time: 10 minutes
Cooking time: about 15 minutes

This dish is a staple in our house. It's so quick to make, inexpensive and delicious! As with so many recipes, you can play around with the ingredients – add strips of semi-dried tomatoes, toss through some fresh chopped dill or basil, or take out the bacon for a simple vegetarian dish.

1 packet (375 g) dried fettuccine
6 bacon rashers (about 500 g), rind removed, cut into thin strips
200 g button mushrooms, finely sliced

2 garlic cloves, crushed
2 tbs Dijon mustard
¼ tsp ground white pepper
300 ml thickened cream

1   Cook the fettuccine in a large saucepan of salted boiling water according to packet directions, or until al dente. Before draining the fettuccine, reserve half a cup of the pasta water.

2   Meanwhile, preheat a non-stick frypan, and sauté the bacon over medium heat until starting to brown. Add the mushrooms and cook for a further 3–4 minutes. Add garlic and continue to cook until it is soft and fragrant.

3   Add the reserved pasta water to the bacon mixture and follow with the mustard and ground white pepper. Add the cream and simmer for 3–4 minutes until the sauce thickens. Taste, and add salt if required, bearing in mind that bacon can be very salty.

4   Stir the drained pasta through the sauce. Serve with freshly grated parmesan and steamed broccoli or a green salad, and garlic bread (page 117).

'My food rule is, "If you don't eat it, I will!".' – Joe

Thai chicken curry

serves 4

Preparation time: 15 minutes
Cooking time: 15 minutes

Mick and I went to Thailand for our honeymoon (many moons ago!). I fell in love with the people, the landscape and the flavours and have sought out good Thai food ever since. This is a simple curry made from scratch with beautiful, fresh ingredients.

2 cups (450 g) jasmine rice
½ bunch coriander
1 stalk lemongrass, white part only, finely chopped
2 small red chillies, seeded and chopped
2 garlic cloves
5 cm piece ginger, peeled and chopped
2 tbs peanut oil
600 g chicken thigh fillets, chopped

2 kaffir lime leaves, finely shredded
400 ml can coconut cream
1 small zucchini, sliced into ribbons
50 g green beans, topped, tailed and sliced
1 tbs brown sugar
2 tsp fish sauce
2 tbs lime juice

1   Place the jasmine rice into a microwave-safe container with 3 cups (750 ml) water. Cover with the lid or seal well with plastic wrap. Microwave on High for 18 minutes, then fluff with a fork.

2   Wash the coriander thoroughly, and scrape the roots with a knife to clean them. Chop the roots and stems (reserve the leaves for serving). Place into a mortar and pestle with the lemongrass, chillies, garlic and ginger, and grind to a paste.

3   Heat ¼ teaspoon peanut oil in a non-stick wok over high heat and quickly stir-fry a quarter of the chicken until starting to brown. Transfer to a bowl and repeat with the remaining oil and chicken.

4   Heat a few drops of oil in the wok and stir-fry the curry paste for 2 minutes, or until fragrant. Return the chicken to the wok and toss to coat in the paste. Add the kaffir lime leaves and coconut cream. Reduce the heat and simmer for 4–5 minutes, or until the chicken is cooked through. In the last minute of cooking, add the zucchini and beans.

5   Add brown sugar, fish sauce and lime juice. Taste, and add more of any of these things as your taste dictates. Serve with the steamed jasmine rice, scattered with coriander leaves.

Slow-cooked lamb shanks

serves 4

Preparation time: 15 minutes
Cooking time: 6–8 hours

I can't think of a more comforting, warming winter dish than lamb shanks
that have been cooked until the soft meat is falling away from the bone and
the whole house is filled with the aroma of the rich, luscious gravy.

½ cup (75 g) plain flour
½ tsp salt
¼ tsp ground white pepper
4 lamb shanks
3 tbs olive oil
2 brown onions, diced
4 garlic cloves, crushed
2 carrots, diced
2 tbs tomato paste
1 cup (250 ml) red wine
2 cups (500 ml) beef stock

2 x 400 g tins chopped tomatoes
2 tbs brown sugar
1 bouquet garni

Gremolata
½ cup flat leaf parsley, finely chopped
1 garlic clove, chopped
1 tbs finely grated lemon zest
¼ tsp cracked black pepper

1 If using the oven, preheat to 160°C (140°C fan-forced). Combine the flour, salt and pepper in a
   snap-lock bag large enough to accommodate one lamb shank. Place a shank into the bag and shake
   to coat well with the flour. Shake off excess flour, and repeat with remaining shanks.

2 Heat 1 tablespoon of the olive oil in a large chef's pan over medium-high heat. Cook the shanks two
   at a time in the pan, turning occasionally, until brown on all sides. Add another tablespoon of oil for
   the second batch. Transfer them to the bowl of the slow cooker. If cooking in the oven, use a large
   oven-proof and flame-proof casserole dish.

3 Reduce the heat to medium and add the onions, garlic and carrots to the pan. Sauté for 2 minutes,
   until the onion is starting to soften. Add the tomato paste and stir for another minute. Add the red
   wine, beef stock, tomatoes, sugar and bouquet garni. Bring to the boil and pour over the shanks.
   Make sure the shanks are submerged.

Continued overleaf ...

4   Cook, covered, for 6–8 hours on low setting in the slow cooker, or for 2–3 hours in the oven. The lamb should be buttery-soft and falling off the bone (see Note).

5   Remove the lamb from the slow cooker and set in a warm place covered in foil. Taste the sauce to see if it needs any further salt. Turn the cooker to the high setting and cook uncovered for around half an hour, or until the sauce thickens slightly. If you have been cooking in the oven, remove the shanks, place the pot onto the stove top and bring sauce to the simmer. If the lamb shanks were particularly fatty you may like to use a ladle to remove some of the fat off the top.

6   To make the gremolata, combine all the ingredients. Serve the shanks swimming in a generous coating of the sauce, with mashed potato and a handful of the gremolata over the top.

Note: I made this dish simultaneously in two different brands of slow cooker. It was very interesting just how different the 'low' settings were from one another. The cooking time varied by about two hours, as one cooker had a much lower heat than the other. It just brings home to me once again how widely equipment (and ingredients, for that matter) can vary, and how important it is to keep an eye out, taste as you go and use your own judgment.

'I love to come home to the sound of the children watching TV or listening to music or playing games and calling out hello, and the smell of dinner cooking ... It's so safe and warm and comforting and there's always a big hug and kiss for the cook.' – Paul

Paddy is a very active 12-year-old, who eats as though he is about to break the height/speed barrier. Which I am sure he would, if there were such a thing.

Recently, he came home from school, stuck his head in the pantry, and proceeded to empty it of the school snacks we had ready for the week. This was followed by cheese and crackers and a whole bag of grapes. He made himself a sandwich, washed it down with milk, then asked why there was nothing in the house to eat. He was like a one-man swarm of locusts descending on a crop.

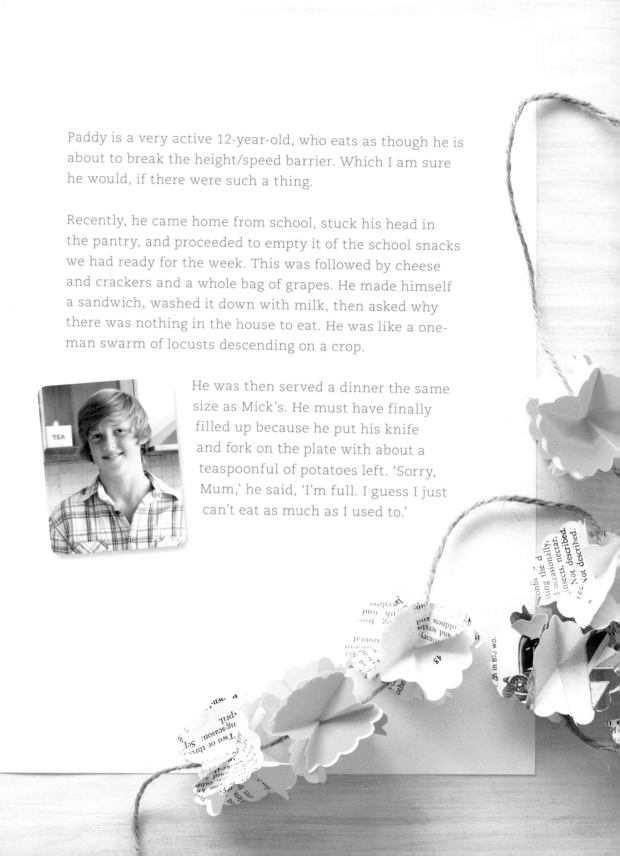

He was then served a dinner the same size as Mick's. He must have finally filled up because he put his knife and fork on the plate with about a teaspoonful of potatoes left. 'Sorry, Mum,' he said, 'I'm full. I guess I just can't eat as much as I used to.'

Barramundi fillet with pineapple salsa

Serves 4

Preparation time: 15 minutes
Cooking time: 5 minutes

This is a very fast, simple meal that is as tasty as it is healthy.

½ fresh pineapple, finely diced
3 small red chillies, seeded and finely sliced
½ small red onion, finely diced
¼ cup coriander leaves, chopped
⅓ cup mint leaves, finely chopped

finely grated zest and juice of 1 lime
1 tbs caster sugar
2 tbs olive oil, extra
25 g butter
4 (approx 1 kg) barramundi fillets, skin on

1   In a medium bowl combine the pineapple, chillies, onion, coriander, mint and lime zest. In a separate bowl stir the lime juice and sugar until the sugar has dissolved. Toss the dressing through the salsa.

2   To cook the barramundi, heat the flat plate of the barbecue (or a chef's pan on the stove) to medium-high and drizzle the oil over. Add the butter – it should foam straight away, and start to go brown, but not burn.

3   Place the fish onto the plate skin side down and cook for 2–3 minutes. Using an egg flip, very carefully turn the fish over. Handle with care so the fish doesn't break up. It should have some lovely golden brown bits. Cook for a further 1–2 minutes and lift carefully onto a serving platter. Serve topped with the pineapple salsa, with steamed rice and Asian greens or salad.

Note: You can make the salsa ahead of time, and refrigerate until needed. Return to room temperature to serve.

*'Michael and I have "date night"– we have a special meal,
with wine, after the kids go to bed.' – Erin*

Beef and red wine pies

serves 6

Preparation time: 30 minutes
Cooking time: 2½ hours

The only way to improve on a beef and wine casserole is to give it a pastry top and call it a pie!
This dish uses very inexpensive cuts of meat – I favour the shin beef because I love the texture
that all the connective tissue creates after a long, slow bath in rich gravy.

½ cup (75 g) plain flour
½ tsp salt
¼ tsp ground white pepper
¼ tsp ground oregano
1.2 kg stewing beef (shin or gravy beef), cut into 3 cm cubes
¼ cup (60 ml) vegetable oil
1 onion, chopped

2 garlic cloves, chopped
2 tbs tomato paste
250 g button mushrooms, sliced
2 tsp thyme leaves
1 cup (250 ml) red wine
1 cup (250 ml) beef stock
3 sheets puff pastry
1 egg, lightly beaten

1 Combine the flour, salt, pepper and oregano in a bowl and toss the meat through. Heat 1 tablespoon
   of the oil in a large chef's pan over high heat. Shake the excess flour from the meat and brown the
   meat in three batches, reheating the pan with a little more oil between batches. Set aside.

2 Reduce the heat to medium and add the last tablespoon of oil. Sauté the onions and garlic until soft
   but not brown. Add the tomato paste and stir for a further minute. Return the meat to the pan, then
   add the mushrooms and thyme. Pour in the red wine followed by the beef stock, stirring and scraping
   the bottom of the pan. Cover and bring to a simmer, then cook over low heat for 2 hours, or until the
   meat is very tender. If the sauce needs to thicken, cook with the lid off for the last 30 minutes.

3 Preheat the oven to 200°C (180°C fan-forced). Ladle the beef into six individual pie dishes or
   ramekins. Don't allow the mixture to be too wet – leave some gravy behind in the pot if you like
   and keep for another meal.

4 Cut rounds from the pastry to fit your pie dishes, allowing a little to hang over the edge. Place the
   pastry over each pie dish and press around the rim. Cut off any excess pastry. Poke a few holes in
   the top with a sharp knife and brush with the egg mixed with 1 tablespoon of water. Bake for 25
   minutes or until puffed and golden.

Note: Use your pie dishes as a guide to cut the pastry tops. This pie is also lovely with a homemade
shortcrust pastry top, done in one large dish rather than individual dishes.

Oven-fried chicken

serves 4

Preparation time: 10 minutes
Cooking time: 30 minutes

We hardly ever ate fast food growing up, so one of the few times we did stands
out in my memory. It was the night of the royal wedding – Charles and Diana.
Dad went out to get Kentucky Fried Chicken (as it used to be called in the days before
everything was turned into an acronym) and hauled the TV into the good lounge room.
It's one of the few times I remember being allowed to eat in front of the telly instead of
around the table! Here's my healthier alternative to deep-fried chicken.

2 cups (80 g) fresh breadcrumbs
½ tsp paprika
¼ tsp garlic powder
¼ tsp ground white pepper

2 tsp salt
1 x 1.6 kg chicken, jointed or 1.6 kg chicken pieces
50 g butter, melted

1   Preheat the oven to 200°C (180°C fan-forced) and line a large baking tray with non-stick
    baking paper.

2   Combine all the ingredients except the chicken and butter in a large bowl. Brush the chicken pieces
    with butter, then dip into the crumb mixture. Press the crumbs firmly to the chicken.

3   Arrange the crumbed chicken onto the prepared tray. Bake for 20 minutes, then turn the chicken
    over and bake for a further 10 minutes (a little longer may be needed for large chicken pieces). The
    crumbs should be golden brown, and the chicken cooked through.

Note: Try adding grated parmesan or sesame seeds to the breadcrumbs. Play around with the spices
in the crumb mixture, or add finely chopped fresh rosemary or basil.

*'All the kids in our house agree – the worst thing about dinner is having to wash
up after Mum has cooked. She's messy.' – Sam, Luke, Lauren and Jess*

4 | Also starring...

It's often the side dishes that make a meal, and they can even be a meal in themselves.

Last year, we went to India and that trip has inspired a few of the dishes in this book. But the trip inspired me in a far more profound way as well. It was in the poorest place I have ever seen, in the harshest living conditions I have ever encountered, that I learned of the concept of *adithi devo bhava* which means: treat your guest like a God.

Mick, the three boys and I joined a group of Aussies from the 40K Foundation, to be present at the opening of a school in Bangalore. The 40K Foundation is an amazing group of young people who have built a magnificent bridging school for the children of a severely underprivileged community of quarry workers.

It was an incredible experience, not only for us to see the amazing colours and sights of India but also to witness firsthand the grinding poverty that so many people suffer.

Clary, the CEO of 40K, had lived and worked in the community to better understand their needs. The village consists of earth-floor huts covered with palm-leaf thatch. There is no running water, no electricity and no sewerage, and the families live, eat and sleep in the tiny space.

One night Clary was invited to share an evening meal with one of the quarry workers, Sinha, his wife Nirmala and their two children, aged 1 and 3. He was welcomed into the hut, given the one straw mat to sit on and had his hands washed from a goblet. He was served a bowl of white rice with sambar, a watery vegetable stew. His bowl was filled to the brim, and no one else in the family ate until he had finished it off. Only then did the family serve themselves – a fraction of the portion they had given Clary.

Clary told me that it was truly humbling to be served with such warmth and selflessness, by people with so very little.

Clary's story, along with our own experiences of this incredible country and community, touched my heart, and will always serve as a reminder, not only of how the sharing of a meal crosses cultural and language barriers, but of what true generosity and graciousness means.

Rocket and pear salad

serves 4 as an accompaniment

Preparation time: 10 minutes

The combination of pears, goats' cheese and white balsamic glaze is so refreshing and lovely. If you don't have white balsamic, there's a recipe overleaf, or you can use dark glaze instead.

150 g rocket leaves
2 shallots, very finely sliced
1 firm pear, cored and cut into fine slices
¼ cup mint leaves, roughly chopped
¼ cup (60ml) white balsamic glaze (store bought, or see overleaf)

¼ cup (60 ml) olive oil
100 g goats' cheese
¼ cup (40 g) pine nuts, toasted
(the little tiny ones if possible)

1   Combine the rocket, shallots, pear and mint in a bowl. Drizzle most of the balsamic glaze and olive oil over, season with salt and pepper to taste and toss through.

2   To assemble the salad, arrange the rocket mixture on serving plates or a platter. Top with crumbled goats' cheese and scatter with pine nuts. Drizzle with the remaining balsamic glaze and olive oil, and serve.

'My grandmothers always impressed on me the importance of pride in my cooking. "Reputation!" they would say in their heavy Greek accents. Cooking is a skill instilled in us at a very young age. Lucky I love it anyway!' – Liane

White balsamic glaze

makes 400 ml

Preparation time: *2 minutes*
Cooking time: 1 hour

I was once given a bottle of white balsamic glaze and I loved it so much I went looking for more. I couldn't find it so I decided to make my own. Balsamic glaze can be made without sugar, just by reducing the vinegar, but I like to use the sugar as it doesn't have to be reduced quite as much to achieve the right consistency. Warning – this will stink the house out!

4 cups (1 litre) white balsamic vinegar   ½ cup (110 g) caster sugar

1   Combine the vinegar and sugar in a medium saucepan, and stir over medium heat without boiling until the sugar has dissolved.

2   Bring to the boil, then reduce the heat and simmer for an hour or until thickened and reduced by about half. Cool and transfer to a clean bottle (the vinegar bottle is ideal). Use as a salad dressing, or drizzle over grilled fish.

'We usually make a big deal about how Lyn has made a beautiful meal for us and we all give her a clap and embarrass her. We tend to do this especially when the kids have friends over.' – Paul

Coleslaw

serves 6–8 as a side dish

Preparation time: 10 minutes

This is a classic, sweet slaw that goes well at a barbecue, picnic or in sandwiches and burgers.

4 cups finely sliced cabbage (about ½ head)
1 small carrot, grated
½ medium white onion, grated
1 cup (250 ml) whole-egg mayonnaise

½ cup (125 ml) tarragon vinegar
2 tbs caster sugar
½ tsp salt
¼ tsp pepper

1   Combine the cabbage, carrot and onion in a large bowl.

2   Mix the mayonnaise, vinegar, sugar, salt and pepper until smooth. Toss through the vegetables. Keep in the fridge, then allow to come to room temperature about 30 minutes before serving.

'The family is the heart of our home – without everyone doing their own thing, whether it is cooking, cleaning, washing, watching TV, playing games or making a mess, then it's just an empty house.' – Mary

'We loved it when Dad did the grocery shopping and bought us all the things we asked Mum for and never got. I don't think Mum loved it.' – Rose

Carrot salad

serves 6 as an accompaniment

Preparation time: 10 minutes

My brother-in-law Anthony learned Ayurvedic cooking and this carrot salad
(and its many variations) is something he made and ate regularly to reduce toxins.
I now make it regularly because it tastes seriously good.

2 large carrots, grated (about 3 cups)
1 cup (80 g) shredded coconut
¾ cup (135 g) raisins
¼ cup (60 ml) white wine vinegar
2 tbs curry powder

¼ cup (60 ml) extra virgin olive oil
1 tsp salt
1 tbs brown sugar
½ cup (70 g) slivered almonds, toasted

1   Combine carrots, coconut and raisins in a bowl.

2   Place the vinegar, curry powder, oil, salt and sugar in a jar and shake vigorously until well
combined.

3   Make sure all ingredients are at room temperature to serve. Up to an hour before serving, pour the
dressing over and toss to combine. Scatter the top with toasted almonds just before serving.

*'Steve and I are very much equals in our kitchen and our home.
Our home is designed so that the children can work and play around the kitchen
while we prepare dinner. This truly makes it the heart of our home.' – Liz*

Also starring …

Spanish corn salad

serves 4 as an accompaniment

Preparation time: 5 minutes
Cooking time: 4 minutes

This is something a little different. It's lovely as an accompaniment
to grilled chicken or as a filling in burritos.

2 fresh corn cobs	¼ cup coriander leaves, chopped
¼ red capsicum, finely chopped	¼ cup (60 g) whole-egg mayonnaise
2 shallots, thinly sliced	splash hot chilli sauce, to taste
1 ripe tomato, diced	salt and ground black pepper

1   Halve the corn cobs and microwave for 4 minutes on High. Allow to cool, then cut the kernels from
the cob. Combine with the capsicum, shallots, tomato and coriander.

2   Combine the mayonnaise with the chilli sauce, and season with salt and ground black pepper.
Dress the corn mixture just before serving.

*'As a young child we used to have a vegie patch. I remember helping
Mum to weed and plant, and water it every afternoon. I used to love
eating the peas and beans straight from the garden.' – Paul*

Roti

makes 8

Preparation time: 10 minutes | Cooking time: about 15 minutes

These flatbreads are so simple to make and are just gorgeous fresh off the grill.

2 cups (300 g) plain flour	1 tsp salt
1 tbs olive oil	a little water

1   Combine the first three ingredients in a bowl and mix well. Add water a little at a time until the mixture forms a firm dough. Knead for a few minutes, until smooth.

2   Divide the dough into 8 pieces. Roll out on a floured work surface until very thin (roughly oval shaped, about 12 x 20 cm). Cook on a pre-heated barbecue, char-grill or heavy-based non-stick frying pan over a medium-high heat until brown on both sides.

Indian spiced cauliflower

serves 4 as an accompaniment
Preparation time: 5 minutes | Cooking time: 15 minutes

As 80 per cent of the people in India are Hindu, much of the food is vegetarian. But no plain or boring vegies – everything bursts with big, vibrant flavours. I tried this dish for the first time only a few months ago and now it's a part of every Indian feast we have!

2 tbs vegetable oil	¼ tsp salt and ¼ tsp pepper
1 tsp ground turmeric	25 g butter
1 tsp ground cumin	½ head cauliflower (about 350 g),
¼ tsp ground chilli	trimmed into small florets
2 tsp nigella seeds	

1   Heat a frying pan over medium heat and add oil and spices. Gently fry for a minute or two or until the spices are fragrant.

2   Put the butter and cauliflower into the pan and stir to thoroughly coat in the spice mixture. Add ¼ cup (60 ml) water, cover and steam for 2 minutes. Remove the cover and stir for another minute or until well mixed and cauliflower is tender.

Also starring …

Onion bhaji

makes about 16

Preparation time: 5 minutes
Cooking time: 15 minutes

These are not only great in an Indian banquet but are great as a snack on their own.

1 cup (150 g) plain flour	1 egg, lightly beaten
1 tsp garlic powder	vegetable oil, to fry
1 tbs ground turmeric	3 large brown onions, finely sliced

1 Combine the flour and spices in a bowl and make a well in the centre. Add the egg and just enough water to make a thick batter, similar in consistency to a pikelet batter.

2 Heat 1 tablespoon of the oil in a frying pan, and gently fry the onions over medium heat until soft and golden. Mix through the batter.

3 Heat more oil in the pan (1 cm deep) and drop spoonfuls of the mixture into it. Only cook four to five at a time. Fry until golden on each side. Drain on paper towels and serve.

'I used to play it safe when ordering at a restaurant. Then I started ordering the meal I thought I would like the least. It broadened my food experience and more often than not, I really enjoyed my dinner.' – Mick

Also starring ...

Smashed potatoes

serves 4

Preparation time: 5 minutes
Cooking time: 30 minutes

No peeling, no slicing – just boil, smash and bake.
These are inelegant to look at but taste great!

12–16 chat (baby) potatoes   sea-salt flakes, to serve
2 tbs olive oil

1   Preheat the oven to 200°C (180°C fan-forced). Cook the potatoes in a large pot of boiling salted water until tender but not too mushy. Drain well.

2   Smash gently, with the flat blade of a knife, a meat mallet or with your hand wrapped in a tea towel, so that the skin splits and the potato is slightly squashed.

3   Toss the potatoes with olive oil, sprinkle with salt and arrange in a single layer on a large baking tray. Bake for 15 minutes, or until they are golden and crispy. Sprinkle with sea salt.

*'I remember Gary making our first evening meal as a married couple.
It was steak, mashed potatoes, peas and gravy.' – Louise*

Garlic and herb bread

serves 6

Preparation time: 5 minutes
Cooking time: 8 minutes

The smell of garlic bread cooking makes me instantly hungry and signals a feast ahead.
Garlic breads vary so widely – and not all are great! For me, it has to be buttery,
have a crispy crust, and a little bit of fresh 'herbiness'.

200 g salted butter, softened but not melted   2 tbs fresh herbs of your choice, chopped finely
3 garlic cloves, crushed   1 loaf Turkish bread

1   Preheat the oven to 180°C (160°C fan-forced). Combine the butter, garlic and herbs in a bowl. Split the Turkish loaf in half horizontally, and spread the butter over both halves.

2   Bake, buttered sides up, on an oven tray for 8 minutes or until the butter has melted and the edges have become golden. Cut into pieces and serve hot.

*'A favourite family saying is: "Love is like bread –
it should be made fresh every day."' – Francine*

*'Steve reckons the quality of the garlic bread is a good
indication of the quality of the meal to come.' – Liz*

Onion rings

serves 4–6 as an accompaniment

Preparation time: 5 minutes
Cooking time: 10 minutes

For the best results when deep frying, I recommend the use of a deep-fryer.
They are thermostatically controlled so the oil is always at the right temperature.
When frying at the correct temperature, very little oil is absorbed into the food.
You can use a frying thermometer in a large saucepan too, but it is harder to
keep the oil at the correct temperature and adjustments will need to be made
throughout the cooking time.

1 cup (150 g) plain flour   vegetable oil, for frying
1⅓ cups (330 ml) beer   sea salt flakes
2 large brown onions

1   Place the flour into a bowl and make a well in the centre. Gradually pour the beer in, stirring until
    well mixed. Slice the onions a little less than 1 cm thick, and separate the slices out into individual
    rings.

2   Fill a deep-fryer to the recommended level with vegetable oil and heat to 190°C. Alternatively, half-
    fill a medium saucepan with vegetable oil and use a kitchen thermometer to gauge the temperature.
    Dip each onion ring into the batter and drop into hot oil. Working quickly, place four–six rings into
    the oil at a time. They will float. Fry for 1–2 minutes and then flip them over and fry for a further
    1–2 minutes or until golden brown.

3   Remove from the oil, drain on paper towel and sprinkle with sea salt. Repeat with the rest of the
    onion rings and serve with steak or burgers.

5 | *Bite-sized delights*

Mum was always throwing dinner parties. Some were finger food, some were sit-down dinners, but for the bigger crowds she would cook a buffet-style feast. The guests would file along the kitchen table piling up their plates and finding a spare spot to sit. There was always a lot of laughter and music, and usually some dancing once the wine flowed. My favourite thing about these parties was waking up before everyone else the next morning and finding leftovers to eat for breakfast.

Probably the most important party Mum ever catered was her own wedding to Dad. It was held at Nan's house and was a huge cold buffet, very much in the style of the times. Whole trout, glazed ham and baked honey chicken were served alongside minted potato salad and Hawaiian coleslaw, complete with pineapple, peanuts and glacé cherries. There were lots of fancy embellishments – celery and carrot curls, radish roses – and pavlova and fruit salad for dessert. More than 50 people attended, and Mum says it was the happiest day of her life besides the days Debbie and I were born. (I think she may be forgetting what actually happens on the day your children are born, but it's a nice thing to say anyway.)

(A brief side note to this story: it was Mum's job to do everything for the wedding except to book the accommodation for the mini honeymoon in Collaroy, which was left to Dad. When they arrived Mum went for a swim in the motel pool, and Dad joined her shortly after. He was surprised to find her being propositioned by a strange man. Dad had accidentally booked their honeymoon in a brothel. Yes, they are still happily married – no, Dad doesn't book the holidays any more.)

So, I come from a party-throwing background and it must be in my blood. Planning and preparing the food for a party is one of the best fun things I can think of to do – second only to enjoying the event itself!

Smoked salmon pâté

makes about 1½ cups

Preparation time: 10 minutes

This is a great summer entertainer. Very quick and easy to make,
it can be served as a dip, or for more elegant finger food, piped onto
mini crostini and topped with some dill leaf tips.

100 g smoked salmon	2 tbs fresh dill
250 g cream cheese	pinch salt and ground white pepper
2 tbs baby capers, rinsed	2 tsp Worcestershire sauce
2 tbs baby gherkins (cornichons)	2 tbs lemon juice

1   Combine all the ingredients in a food processor and process until smooth. Taste, and add more salt or pepper if required.

2   Serve with toasted baguette rounds.

*'My idea of the best-ever party – fancy dress, lots of yummy nibbles,
lots of champagne, loud music and dancing. Karaoke optional.' – Erin*

Mini crostini with salsa

makes 40

Preparation time: 5 minutes
Cooking time: 15 minutes

These little crostini are a great base for any number of toppings.
They are just the right size to pop into your mouth.

10 slices white bread, crusts removed
⅓ cup (80 ml) olive oil, plus a little extra to drizzle
100 g freshly grated parmesan

4 ripe Roma tomatoes, seeded and finely diced
½ bunch fresh basil, chopped

1 Preheat oven to 160°C (140°C fan-forced) and line a baking tray with non-stick baking paper. Using a 4 cm round biscuit cutter, cut four circles from each slice of bread. Lay on the tray and brush generously with olive oil. Turn over and brush other side. Bake for 15 minutes or until golden brown.

2 Place small pinches (about 1 teaspoon) of freshly grated parmesan on a lined tray and bake for 15 minutes or until melted and lightly golden. Cool on the tray until firm.

3 Combine the diced tomato and basil in a bowl, and season with salt and pepper. Drizzle with a little olive oil.

4 Spoon the salsa onto each crostini, and top with a parmesan crisp. Serve immediately.

Other suggested toppings
- Smoked salmon pâté (page 122)
- Chicken liver pâté – remove aspic/jelly from store-bought pâté and pipe onto crostini. Top with a cherry tomato quarter and a grind of black pepper.
- Onion jam and goats' cheese
- Rare roast beef and horseradish

Experiment with anything you like!

Oysters natural

each topping is enough for at least 1 dozen oysters

I am a relative newcomer to the joys of oysters, but now that I have been converted,
I can't get enough of them. The best I have ever eaten were fresh Wagonga Inlet oysters
grown by the Maidment family. We were holidaying a couple of doors up the street from them,
and arrived home from the beach one day to find a huge string bag of plump, juicy and
flavoursome oysters. Dad shucked them and we all hooked in. Below are some very
simple serving ideas for natural oysters; but I have to say, when they are perfectly
fresh and shucked on the spot, they are amazing completely naked.

Naked
Just serve on a bed of salt or crushed ice, with lemon and lime wedges.

Mignonette dressing
Combine ½ cup (125 ml) red wine vinegar, 2 very finely diced brown shallots, and a grind of white
peppercorns. Allow to mellow for a few hours before spooning over natural oysters.

Wasabi and sweet soy
Combine ½ cup (125 ml) light soy sauce and 2 teaspoons palm sugar or brown sugar. Spoon a small
amount over each oyster, and top with a dab of wasabi paste.

Spicy salsa
Combine 1 seeded and very finely diced ripe tomato, 1 seeded and very finely chopped small red chilli
and 2 very finely chopped shallots with lime juice, salt and pepper to taste.

Allow to sit for an hour or so, then spoon a small amount onto each oyster to serve.

Posh
For a real treat, serve each oyster with a small spoonful of salmon roe on top.

'My party philosophy – don't worry about the mess.
Enjoy the night and we'll fix it up tomorrow.' – Marcus

Vietnamese rice paper rolls with dipping sauce

makes 8

Preparation time: 20 minutes
Cooking time: 1 minute

One of the best experiences from our trip to Vietnam was taking a cooking lesson at the Red Bridge cooking school. We made our own fresh rice paper from rice which is soaked, ground, then steamed on a cotton-covered pot. The rolls were filled with prawns and fresh herbs and vegetables from the school's own gardens. It was like eating a little piece of heaven. My recipe uses the store-bought rice paper – fill it with the freshest produce you can for a taste of Vietnam.

Dipping sauce
2 tbs sugar
1½ tbs lime juice
2 tbs fish sauce
1 garlic clove, chopped
2 small red (birdseye) chillies, seeded and chopped

Spring rolls
1 tsp peanut or vegetable oil
100 g green prawn meat, chopped

1 pinch each sugar and salt
1 Lebanese cucumber
½ cup (40 g) bean sprouts
½ cup (60 g) grated carrot
4 shallots, sliced finely lengthways
2 tsp lime juice
1 pinch each sugar and salt, extra
8 large rice paper wrappers
½ cup (30 g) lettuce leaves, shredded
½ cup mixed fresh herbs, chopped (see Note)

1   In a bowl combine the sugar, lime juice and fish sauce. Stir to dissolve the sugar, then add the garlic and chilli. Taste and add more sugar or fish sauce if desired.

2   For the spring rolls, heat the oil in a wok over medium heat. Add the prawn meat, sugar and salt and stir-fry for 1 minute or until cooked. Transfer to a plate to cool.

3   Halve the cucumber, then remove the seeds by scraping a teaspoon along the centre. Grate into a clean tea towel or paper towel, then wring out all the moisture. Toss with the bean sprouts, carrot, shallots, lime juice, sugar and salt.

4   To assemble the rolls, dip one sheet of rice paper into warm water and rest on a damp cloth. Arrange one eighth of the lettuce and herbs in a line along the lower third of the wrapper followed by one eighth of the salad mixture and one eighth of the prawn mixture. Fold the ends over and roll the paper tightly. Place the roll on a damp cloth and cover with another damp cloth to prevent drying out. Repeat for the remaining seven rolls.

5   To serve, cut the rolls in half and place on a platter with a small dish of dipping sauce.

Note: Use a mixture of herbs, such as coriander, Vietnamese mint, common mint and basil.

Lamb meatballs with yoghurt dipping sauce

makes 90

Preparation time: 20 minutes
Cooking time: 6 minutes per batch

These little meatballs pack a big flavour punch.
They are an absolute hit at parties – nobody can stop at one.

1 tbs olive oil	750 g lamb mince
1 small onion, finely diced	1 egg
2 garlic cloves, crushed	olive oil, for cooking
1 tbs ground coriander	1 cup (250 g) natural yoghurt
1 tbs ground cumin	1 cup finely shredded mint
¼ tsp ground chilli	2 tsp lemon juice
½ cup (80 g) pine nuts, toasted and roughly chopped	2 tsp maple syrup

1   Heat the oil in a large frying pan, and cook the onion and garlic over medium heat, until translucent but not brown. Place into a large bowl. Stir in the spices and pine nuts, then add the lamb and egg. Spend a good few minutes working the ingredients into the lamb, kneading with your hands. It is important to massage the meat quite vigorously, until it is sticky.

2   Roll small portions into balls, about the size of a walnut. Heat 1 teaspoon olive oil in the frying pan over medium heat. Cook the meatballs, turning regularly, until they are browned and cooked through – about 6 minutes. Drain on paper towels. Repeat until all meatballs are cooked.

3   Meanwhile, combine the yoghurt, mint, lemon juice and maple syrup in a small bowl. Season with freshly ground black pepper. Serve the meatballs on a platter with toothpicks, and the yoghurt dipping sauce on the side.

*'The finger food I remember is chicken chips, pies, sausage rolls
and meatballs. I especially loved the meatballs.' – Paul*

Chicken satay

makes 60 canapé-sized skewers

Preparation time: 20 minutes
Cooking time: 10–15 minutes

Tom, my middle son, loves chicken satay and asks for it all the time.
This sauce recipe is one we came up with together.

6 chicken breast fillets (about 1.5 kg)
½ bunch coriander
1 brown onion, diced
4 garlic cloves, crushed
2 limes, zest finely grated, juiced
1 long red chilli, seeds removed, chopped
1 tbs peanut oil

1 tsp ground turmeric
¼ tsp chilli powder
400 ml tin coconut cream
1 cup (280 g) crunchy peanut butter
¼ cup (60 ml) fish sauce
¼ cup (50 g) brown sugar
iceberg lettuce leaves

1   Soak 60 small bamboo skewers in water for at least an hour.

2   Cut the breast fillets into about 10 strips each, along the grain. Thread one strip onto each skewer, weaving in and out a few times so the chicken is secure.

3   Wash the roots and stems of the coriander (keep the leaves for garnish) and place into a food processor along with the onion, garlic, lime zest and chilli. Process until very finely chopped (alternatively, crush in a mortar and pestle).

4   Heat the oil in a large non-stick frypan over medium heat. Add the onion mixture and fry until soft and fragrant. Be careful not to let it 'catch' or start to burn. Add the turmeric and chilli powder and stir for a further minute or so. Add half the coconut cream and all the peanut butter, and bring to a simmer for 5 minutes or so. The sauce will split – this is okay.

5   Reduce the heat to low and add the fish sauce, brown sugar and half the lime juice. Taste to see if the sauce needs any more of these three things. (This is very dependent on personal taste.) Stir in the rest of the coconut cream, taste again and adjust seasoning if need be. Remove from heat.

6   Preheat a barbecue grill or a char-grill plate on the stove to a medium-high heat. Cooking a few at a time, grill the chicken until just cooked through. The time will depend on how tightly the chicken is threaded onto the skewer and how thick the pieces are. Being breast chicken it will dry out easily, so be careful not to overcook.

7   To serve, place the skewer onto a trimmed iceberg lettuce leaf, smother with sauce and top with coriander leaves.

Sang choy bow

makes about 3 cups of mixture –
the serving sizes will determine how many portions

Preparation time: 5 minutes
Cooking time: 10 minutes

Every time we order Chinese food, sang choy bow is on the list; it's a family favourite.
Making it for parties is cheap and easy.

1 tbs peanut oil

1 brown onion, finely chopped

2 garlic cloves, finely chopped

3 cm piece ginger, finely grated (about 1 tbs)

1 small red chilli, deseeded and finely chopped

500 g pork mince

1 x 230 g tin water chestnuts, drained and chopped

1 tsp sesame oil

2 tbs oyster sauce

2 tbs soy sauce

2 tsp cornflour

3 shallots, finely sliced

8 iceberg lettuce leaves, washed and trimmed

1 cup (80 g) bean sprouts

2 tbs toasted sesame seeds

1   Heat the oil in a frying pan over medium heat, and add the onion, garlic, ginger and chilli and stir-fry until soft and fragrant.

2   Add the mince and stir to break up any lumps as it cooks. Add the water chestnuts, followed by the sesame oil, and oyster and soy sauces.

3   Dissolve the cornflour in ¼ cup (60 ml) water and add to the pan. Stir for another couple of minutes until the mixture thickens slightly.

4   Take the pan off the heat and stir through the shallots. Serve a generous spoonful on a lettuce leaf, topped with bean sprouts and sprinkled with sesame seeds.

*'My idea of the best-ever party is being surrounded by loved ones,
enjoying finger food and dancing to good music.' – Tony*

Arancini balls

makes about 30 bite-sized balls

Preparation time: 30 minutes
Cooking time: 1 hour

I admit it – these are fiddly to make.
But once your guests get a taste of the rich creamy filling,
crisp exterior and melty cheese centre, you will be glad you went to the effort.

4 cups (1 litre) chicken stock	1 cup (80 g) freshly ground parmesan
50 g butter	salt and ground white pepper
1 tbs olive oil	vegetable oil for deep-frying
1 brown onion, finely diced	2 tbs basil, finely chopped
2 garlic cloves, finely chopped	2 eggs, lightly beaten
1½ cups (330 g) arborio rice	150 g knob mozzarella, cut into 1 cm cubes
½ cup (125 ml) white wine	2 cups (80 g) fresh breadcrumbs

1   Bring the chicken stock to a simmer in a medium saucepan. Stir the butter and olive oil in a large saucepan over medium heat until the butter is melted. Add the onion and garlic and sauté until soft. Add the rice and stir until the grains start to become transparent. Pour in the wine and cook until it has been absorbed into the rice.

2   Stir in the hot stock a ladleful at a time, waiting for the liquid to be absorbed after each addition. This will happen quite quickly initially, but will slow down as the rice becomes more saturated. Stir gently to make sure that the rice isn't sticking to the bottom of the pot, but do not break up the grains of rice. When the liquid is absorbed and the risotto has a creamy consistency, taste a few of the grains to make sure they are cooked. They should have some substance to them, but not have any hint of hardness in the centre.

3   Stir in the parmesan, then taste and add salt and pepper to your liking. It will not need much salt as the parmesan is quite salty. Cool the rice mixture in the fridge.

4   Fill a deep-fryer to the recommended level with vegetable oil and heat to 180°C. Alternatively, half-fill a medium saucepan with vegetable oil and use a kitchen thermometer for temperature.

Continued next page ...

Arancini balls *continued ...*

Meanwhile, add the basil and eggs to the rice, and mix well. Take a golf-ball-sized piece of the rice mixture and roll into a ball. Press a cube of mozzarella into the centre of the rice, and roll the ball in breadcrumbs. Repeat with the remaining ingredients.

5   Deep-fry the balls in batches for 3 minutes, or until crispy and deep golden brown. Drain on paper towels and serve while hot. These are lovely served on their own, but also beautiful with a sweet tomato sauce or cranberry sauce.

Note: Save stale bread in the freezer to make breadcrumbs with. Once the bread is crumbed it can be frozen as well, and will keep for around 3 months.

'Best-ever party would be somewhere overlooking the ocean,
being served great finger food and cocktails and, of course, great
music (maybe a bit of ABBA).' – Mary

A Blast from the Past –
Mum's '70s Canapé Menu

- Toothpicks with cubes of cheese and orange segments
- Toothpicks with cubes of cheese and green or red cocktail onions
- Toothpicks with cubes of cheese and gherkin
- Toothpicks with cubes of cheese and rockmelon
- Crustless buttered bread wrapped around an asparagus spear (secured with a toothpick)
- Mashed potato with diced raw onion wrapped in a slice of devon (secured with a toothpick)
- Devilled eggs. (No toothpick!)

One of Mum's famous spreads – this one is for Deb's birthday.

Sausage rolls

makes 96 cocktail sausage rolls

Preparation time: 10 minutes
Cooking time: 25 minutes

The quantity in this recipe is pretty huge – if there are too many for your gathering,
they can be frozen before they are baked and used another time.

1 kg good quality sausage mince	¼ cup (60 g) French mustard
500 g beef mince	2 tbs curry powder
2 brown onions, grated	1 tsp salt
2 carrots, grated	½ tsp pepper
2 cups (80 g) fresh breadcrumbs	6 sheets frozen puff pastry
½ cup (125 ml) tomato sauce	1 egg

1   Preheat oven to 200°C (180°C fan-forced). Line 2 large baking trays with non-stick baking paper.
Place all ingredients except for the pastry and egg in a large bowl. Using your hands, work the
mixture very well until all combined.

2   Lay the pastry out on a work surface and cut each sheet in half. Divide the sausage mixture into
12 portions and lay in a line along the length of each pastry half-sheet. Fold the two sides over the
sausage mixture and gently press to join.

3   Turn the rolls over, and cut each one into eight pieces. Place seam side down onto the baking trays
and brush with the egg that has been beaten with 1 tablespoon water. Bake for 20–25 minutes until
pastry is puffed and golden.

*'We think our Greek food is normal ... until we take it to school! I used to want Vegemite
sandwiches in my lunchbox. Now I am proud of our beautiful food.' – Liane*

Mini quiche Lorraine

makes 12

Preparation time: 15 minutes
Cooking time: 25 minutes

These are a larger sized finger food, possibly for a more casual party than for an elegant, refined affair. Loved by kids and adults alike, they are great for a picnic too.

3 sheets frozen puff pastry
4 rashers bacon, rind removed, finely diced
6 shallots, white and pale green parts only, sliced
1 cup (100 g) grated tasty cheese

6 eggs, lightly beaten
⅓ cup (80 ml) milk
¼ tsp salt
¼ tsp ground white pepper

1 Preheat the oven to 200ºC (180ºC fan-forced). Using a 9 cm round cookie cutter, cut four circles of partially thawed pastry from each sheet. Place the circles into a 12-hole non-stick cupcake tray (¼ cup (60 ml) capacity). Press neatly into each hole.

2 Sauté the bacon in a small non-stick frying pan over medium heat until just starting to brown. Remove from the heat and allow to cool. Stir through the shallots.

3 Divide half the grated cheese between the 12 cases. Top with the bacon and shallot mixture, then the remaining cheese. Combine eggs, milk, salt and pepper in a jug. Pour slowly and carefully into the pastry cases.

4 Bake for 20 minutes or until the top is golden brown and the pastry is cooked. (The quiches will puff up quite a lot during cooking but will subside once they cool down a bit.) Trim off any untidy bits that have spilled over during cooking before serving. Serve warm or at room temperature.

Note: Instead of bacon and shallots, try asparagus and smoked salmon, or sautéed mushrooms and semi-dried tomatoes, or spinach and sautéed onion.

Maria's spinach pastries

makes 50

Preparation time: 20 minutes
Cooking time: 20 minutes

This recipe was generously shared with me by Maria, along with many other of her authentic Greek recipes. Maria says, 'The heart of my home is my family – my children, grandchildren and husband'.

Pastry	Filling
5 cups (750 g) plain flour	250 g baby spinach leaves
pinch salt	100 g feta, crumbled
1 tbs white wine vinegar	100 g parmesan cheese, grated
1 cup (250 ml) olive oil	250 g ricotta cheese
1 egg yolk	3 eggs, lightly beaten
1 tbs milk	1 tsp salt
	½ tsp ground black pepper
	¼ tsp nutmeg

1 Preheat oven to 180°C (160°C fan-forced). Line a baking tray with non-stick baking paper. Blanch the spinach briefly in salted boiling water. Drain well, and press the excess moisture out with a clean tea towel. Chop the leaves.

2 To make the pastry, place the flour and salt into a large bowl and make a well in the centre. Add the vinegar, oil and 1½ cups (375 ml) warm water, and mix with a wooden spoon and then your hands to form a smooth dough. Roll out to 2 mm thick and cut into circles with a 9 cm round cutter.

3 For the filling, mix the spinach with the other ingredients until evenly combined. To assemble, place a slightly heaped teaspoon of filling into the centre of each pastry circle. Fold the dough over to enclose and make a semi-circle, and press the edges together with a fork.

4 Brush with the combined egg yolk and milk, and place onto the tray. Bake for 20 minutes, until golden brown.

Andrea's pork and prawn wontons

makes 100–120

Preparation time: 1 hour
Cooking time: 10 minutes

This is another recipe from Andrea. She makes these in bulk with my brother-in-law and they freeze them raw, making it the ideal do-ahead party dish. Defrost, fry, and serve – delicious.

500 g peeled and deveined green prawns, very finely chopped
500 g pork mince (not too lean)
1 tbs finely grated ginger
2 tsp sugar
⅓ cup (80 ml) light soy sauce
⅓ cup (80 ml) Shaoxing cooking wine (or dry sherry)

1 tsp sesame oil
2 tbs cornflour, plus extra for dusting
6 shallots, finely chopped
1 tsp each salt and white pepper
100–120 yellow square wonton wrappers
vegetable oil, to deep fry

1   For the filling, combine prawn, pork, ginger, sugar, soy sauce, wine, sesame oil, cornflour and shallots. Season with the salt and pepper and mix well with clean hands, until well combined.

2   Work with a few wontons at a time and keep the rest covered with a damp cloth. Place a teaspoon of filling into the centre of the square wonton and brush the edges with water. Gather all the corners to the centre and twist firmly to enclose filling.

3   Repeat with remaining wrappers and filling. Lightly dust the wontons with cornflour and leave to dry for about 1 hour. They can be frozen at this stage.

4   To cook the wontons, fill a deep-fryer to the recommended level with vegetable oil and heat to 180°C. Alternatively, half-fill a large saucepan or wok with vegetable oil and use a kitchen thermometer for temperature. Cook the wontons in batches for 2–3 minutes, turning halfway through, until golden and the filling is cooked through. Make sure not to put too many in the pot at once or the temperature of the oil will drop and they will be oily. Remove with a slotted spoon and drain on paper towels. Serve with sweet chilli sauce.

Thai-style fish cakes

makes about 45

Preparation time: 15 minutes
Cooking time: about 5 minutes per batch

This Thai delicacy is another lovely memory from my honeymoon.
They only take moments to prepare, and are bite-sized flavour bombs.

500 g boneless, skinless white fish fillets
1 egg, beaten
¼ cup (35 g) cornflour
1 tbs fish sauce
1 tbs red curry paste

2 tbs cleaned, chopped coriander roots and stems
1 small red chilli, finely chopped
8 green beans, sliced
4 shallots, sliced
peanut oil, for frying

1   Process the fish in a food processor until almost smooth, then transfer to a bowl. Add the egg, cornflour, fish sauce, curry paste, coriander, chilli, beans and shallots and mix well.

2   Take level tablespoons of the mixture and form into small flattened balls. Heat about 1 cm of peanut oil in a frying pan. Cook the fish cakes in batches over medium-high heat for about 1–2 minutes each side, until golden brown. Drain on paper towels.

3   Serve with sweet chilli sauce.

'Our home in Zimbabwe was always full of people; my parents were great entertainers and provided lots and lots of wholesome home-cooked food.' – Nikki

6 | Happy endings

Desserts are no longer the nightly offering they used to be when my parents' generation (and quite a lot of mine) were growing up. I am not sure whether it's because of health concerns, or less time in the kitchen, or simply that we now have enough food to feed the kids for a main meal and don't need to 'fill them up' afterwards. It's not necessarily a bad thing; for one, it removes the dilemma of having to think up two courses for dinner every night!

It's still lovely, though, to finish a meal with a dessert, whether it's a special occasion or just one of those weekdays where there's a little time to spare.

Once when the boys were very little, our oven broke down. As is the case for many young families, we just didn't have the money spare to get it fixed straight away. It felt like losing a limb – not only could I not make our family's favourite roast dinners, but I couldn't bake cakes either!

So when a cake was called for (and let's face it, that happens quite a lot), I had to buy it. Fortunately, we lived only a stone's throw from the Sara Lee factory, so I would splash out on their giant slab cake – they were about two feet long and fed a hungry crowd very nicely.

Joe, who was about 6 at the time, wanted to know why I was buying cakes instead of making them myself. I told him that Sara Lee made the best cakes. He accepted that as a fair enough answer.

Not long afterwards we attended a big family gathering. My sister-in-law Lyn had brought a beautiful homemade chocolate cake. Joe had it all over his face when he marched up to Aunty Lyn and declared, 'My Mum says Sara Lee makes the best cakes.'

It looked like it was going to be one of those moments where we had to step in and apologise for the unintended rudeness of one of our children, when he looked hard at her and asked, 'Are you Sara Lee?'

Profiteroles

makes 24

Preparation time: 40 minutes
Cooking time: 1 hour + cooling time

I have always loved choux pastry. When I was a kid Mum would sometimes buy us a chocolate éclair, which was just the greatest treat. But I had never cooked choux pastry myself, always believing it was tricky, until I had to make a croquembouche on MasterChef. Talk about a steep learning curve! It was a daunting experience but one I am very glad I went through because now I can make one of my favourite desserts of all time.

Choux puffs	Crème pâtissière filling
120 g butter, cubed	2 cups (440 g) caster sugar
¼ tsp salt	10 egg yolks
1½ cups (225 g) plain flour	1 cup (150 g) plain flour
5 eggs, lightly beaten	4 cups (1 litre) milk
	1½ tsp vanilla extract
	3 strips lemon peel
	50 g butter
	1 cup (250 ml) thickened cream
	250 g dark choc bits

1   To make the choux puffs, preheat the oven to 200ºC (180ºC fan-forced). Line 2 baking trays with non-stick baking paper. In a medium saucepan over medium-high heat, bring 1½ cups of water to the boil with the butter and salt. Remove from the heat and add the flour, beating hard with a wooden spoon. Return to low heat for about 5 minutes, constantly stirring, until the dough forms into a ball around the spoon and comes away from the sides of the pan.

2   Remove from the heat and beat with a whisk to speed the cooling process. When the mixture has cooled to a little above room temperature, beat in the eggs a little bit at a time. The mixture should be smooth, glossy and thick. Place the mixture into a large piping bag with a 1 cm plain nozzle. Pipe little piles of mixture, about 4 cm in diameter and 3 cm high, onto the prepared trays. There should be about 24. With a wet finger, smooth down any little peaks on top of the puffs.

Continued overleaf ...

Profiteroles *continued ...*

3   Place into the oven for 10 minutes, then swap the top and bottom trays and cook for a further 10 minutes. Reduce the heat to 160°C (140°C fan-forced) and bake for another 30–40 minutes. The puffs should be golden brown and hollow in the centre. To help prevent the puffs from dropping, make a hole in the bottom straight away with a small sharp knife (or use a very small piping nozzle), and sit the puffs upside down. This will allow air into the puffs, release any steam and help to dry out the insides.

4   To make the crème pâtissière, place the sugar and the egg yolks into the bowl of an electric mixer and beat for 5 minutes on high speed until light and creamy. Add the flour and beat for a further minute until well combined.

5   In a large saucepan, bring milk to the boil with the vanilla and lemon peel. Remove the peel and pour the milk over the egg mixture in a steady stream, beating on low speed. Return the mixture to the saucepan and bring to the boil. Reduce the heat to low and stir continuously with a whisk. The custard will thicken and darken to a yellow colour. Continue to stir for 4–5 minutes or until the flour has cooked out to ensure it doesn't taste raw. Remove from the heat and allow to cool for a few minutes. (To speed the process you can beat with a whisk.) While still slightly warm, beat through the butter. Place into a shallow tray and cover the surface with plastic wrap to avoid a skin forming on top. Refrigerate until you are ready to fill the profiteroles.

6   To fill, place the crème pâtissière into a piping bag with a 4 mm nozzle. Insert the nozzle into the hole on the bottom of each puff and fill slowly and carefully, until the profiterole has a decent weight and you feel resistance when piping.

7   Bring the cream to scalding point in a small saucepan or in the microwave and pour over the choc bits. Stir until melted and smooth. Serve the profiteroles with whipped cream or vanilla ice cream, topped with the warm chocolate sauce.

Note: To serve the profiteroles as a finger food dessert instead of a plated dessert, simply melt the chocolate without the cream, and dip the top of each profiterole in it. Allow the chocolate to cool and harden before serving.

I fell in love with Mick hook, line, sinker – and mullet.

'Eating great food has always been one of the ways we have enjoyed time together. I remember our first Valentine's Day. Jules' parents went out for the night so that she could cook me a romantic dinner. She made her huge cheesy lasagne and bought Coronas. She knew the way to my heart. It was a memorable evening.' – Mick

Apple almond crumble

serves 4–6

Preparation time: 10 minutes
Cooking time: 35 minutes

The smell of cinnamon and apples drifting through the house awakens memories of the crumbles and custard I enjoyed when I was young. This dessert was probably so popular because it was very inexpensive.

6 medium or 8 small Granny Smith apples
¼ cup (55 g) caster sugar
½ tsp ground cinnamon
½ cup (75 g) plain flour

¼ cup (55 g) caster sugar, extra
80 g butter
1 cup (110 g) slivered almonds

1 Preheat the oven to 180°C (160°C fan-forced). Peel, quarter and slice the apples. Place into a medium saucepan with caster sugar, cinnamon and 2 tablespoons water. Simmer for 5 minutes, or until the apples are soft.

2 Combine the flour, extra sugar, butter and three-quarters of the almonds in a food processor and process until just combined.

3 Spread the apples over the base of a 22 cm pie dish. Scatter the crumble mixture over the top and top with the remaining almonds. Press down.

4 Bake for 30 minutes, or until golden on top. The top will still be soft but will crisp up as it cools. Serve with custard, cream or ice cream.

Note: Substitute allspice for cinnamon with the apples, if you like. You could also add desiccated coconut to the crumble mix, or substitute rolled oats for the almonds.

'Love is the heart of our home.' – Kelly

Sticky date pudding with butterscotch sauce

serves 8–12

Preparation time: 20 minutes
Cooking time: about 30 minutes

This was Mick's favourite dessert for years and he would order it almost every time we went out to eat. When I first made it, he was confused as to why I was putting dates in it – he doesn't like them. I asked him what he thought would be in a sticky date pudding. It hadn't occurred to him that it might be dates!

60 g butter
¾ cup (150 g) brown sugar
¼ cup (60 ml) golden syrup
2 eggs
1⅓ cups (200 g) self-raising flour
200 g dates, pitted
300 ml boiling water
1 tsp bicarbonate of soda

Butterscotch sauce
150 ml thickened cream
60 g butter
¼ cup (50 g) brown sugar
¼ cup (60 ml) golden syrup

1   Preheat the oven to 200°C (180°C fan-forced) and grease a 20 cm round cake tin. Using electric beaters, cream the butter and sugar in a large bowl until light. Beat in the golden syrup and eggs. Add the flour a little at a time and beat until combined.

2   Place the dates and boiling water into a food processor and blitz to a purée. Add the bicarb soda, and pour immediately into the batter (it will be quite loose and pale). Pour into the tin and bake for 30 minutes, or until golden brown and lightly springy in the middle. Turn out onto a wire rack.

3   For the butterscotch sauce, place all the ingredients into a saucepan and bring to the boil. Boil for 3 minutes then transfer to a serving jug. Serve the pudding warm, with good quality vanilla ice cream.

No-bake chocolate cheesecake

serves 12

Preparation time: 30 minutes + chilling time

This is an embarrassingly huge cheesecake, and is very rich as well,
so it may not all get eaten in one sitting. The good news is, it freezes well,
and can even be eaten semi-frozen if you can't wait!

250 g packet plain biscuits	500 g milk cooking chocolate, chopped
100 g butter, melted	500 g cream cheese
1 tbs caster sugar	395 g tin condensed milk
1½ tsp powdered gelatine	1 cup (250 ml) thickened cream, whipped

1   Process the biscuits to a rough crumb, similar to breadcrumbs. Add the butter and sugar and mix
well. Press firmly into the base of a 26 cm springform cake tin and refrigerate.

2   Sprinkle the gelatine over ⅔ cup (165 ml) lukewarm water, and stir until dissolved.

3   Place the chocolate into a glass bowl and stand over a pot of barely simmering water. Stir until the
chocolate is just melted, and remove from the heat. (Alternatively, microwave on High for 1 minute,
stir, microwave 1 further minute and stir again.)

4   In the bowl of an electric mixer, beat the cream cheese and melted chocolate until light and fluffy.
With the mixer running, pour in the condensed milk. Remove the bowl from the mixer and stir
through the gelatine mixture, then fold through the whipped cream. Pour into the springform pan.
Refrigerate for several hours (preferably overnight) until set.

*'When Steve and I started going out he was amused that I would
eat the most "valuable" or tasty things on my plate first. He should try
having three older brothers picking the food off your plate every dinner time.'* – Liz

Lemon lime tart

serves 12

Preparation time: 20 minutes
Cooking time: 35 minutes + chilling time

Any dessert with lemon in it gets my vote.
The lime in this tart gives it that extra little zing.

Base	Filling
1½ cups (225 g) plain flour	½ cup (125 ml) lemon juice (about 2 lemons)
¼ cup (40 g) self-raising flour	¼ cup (60 ml) lime juice (about 2 limes)
pinch salt	1 cup (220 g) caster sugar
½ cup (75 g) icing mixture	⅔ cup (160 ml) thickened cream
100 g butter	5 eggs, lightly beaten
1 egg	

1 Preheat the oven to 180°C (160°C fan-forced). Grease a 25 cm fluted loose-based flan tin. (My flan tin has holes in the base, which helps the pastry to crisp on the bottom.)

2 To make the base, place the flours, salt, icing mixture and butter into a food processor. Process in short bursts until it looks like breadcrumbs. Add the egg and process again until the dough comes together in a ball. Turn out onto a board. If the dough seems very dry and crumbly, add a teaspoon of cold water and briefly knead it in. Wrap in plastic wrap and put into the fridge for 15 minutes.

3 Remove the pastry from the fridge and roll out to about 5 mm thick. The pastry is very short – it will be very difficult to move in one piece. Tear pieces from the pastry and, bit by bit, cover the base and sides of the flan tin. Press the edges of the pastry pieces together, taking care to keep it the same thickness throughout. Put a sheet of baking paper into the flan tin and fill with baking weights or rice. Bake for 10 minutes, then remove the baking paper and weights and bake for a further 10 minutes, or until lightly golden brown.

4 Combine the juice, sugar and cream in a bowl. Whisk in the beaten eggs a bit at a time until they are mixed in. Pour the mixture into the pastry case and bake for 25 minutes or until set. Serve at room temperature, or refrigerate until needed and serve chilled. It's beautiful with vanilla ice cream.

Tom's baked caramel cheesecake

serves 12

Preparation time: 20 mins
Cooking time: 35 mins + chilling time

This is similar to the New York-style baked cheesecake, but with the added richness of caramel. It's named for Tom because he always requests it for his birthday.

Base
250 g packet Butternut Snap Cookies
½ cup (60 g) ground almonds
¼ tsp ground nutmeg
125 g butter, melted

Filling
2 cups (440 g) caster sugar
750 g cream cheese, at room temperature
2 eggs
1 tsp vanilla extract

Topping
1 cup (250 g) sour cream
¼ cup (55 g) caster sugar
½ tsp vanilla extract

1 Preheat the oven to 180°C (160°C fan-forced). To make the base, blitz the biscuits in a food processor until they are a fine crumb. Transfer to a large bowl and mix through ground almond and nutmeg. Pour the butter in and mix well.

2 Press the crumb mixture firmly into a 22 cm non-stick springform cake tin. Bring the mixture about 4 cm up the sides of the pan. Chill in the fridge while making the filling.

3 In a medium saucepan, place the caster sugar and ½ cup (125 ml) water. Stir over low heat without boiling to dissolve the sugar, then bring to the boil over a medium heat. Boil without stirring or agitating the pot for about 10 minutes, or until the syrup has darkened to a rich golden colour.

4 Remove from the heat and immediately add 250 g of the cream cheese. Be careful, as this will cause the mixture to froth up. Stir continually until it has melted and is combined with the caramel. Place the caramel mixture in the bowl of an electric mixer with the remaining cream cheese. Beat until very well combined. Add the eggs one at a time, beating well after each addition. Beat in the vanilla. Pour the mixture into the chilled base and bake for 25 minutes.

5 To make the topping, remove the cheesecake from the oven and increase the temperature to 200°C (180°C fan-forced). Combine the sour cream, caster sugar and vanilla and pour over the cheesecake. Return to the oven for 10 minutes. Cool slightly, then refrigerate for 6 hours before serving.

Note: If you don't have 6 hours, chill the cheesecake for half an hour in the freezer before refrigerating.

Brandy-snap baskets with strawberries and mascarpone

serves 4-6

Preparation time: 20 minutes
Cooking time: 20 minutes

These are quite delicate and may take a bit of practice before getting them just right. But it's worth it. Instead of the mascarpone filling, you can experiment with liqueur flavoured creams or vary the fruit.

1 punnet strawberries, sliced
3 tbs caster sugar
50 g butter, cubed
¼ cup (60 ml) golden syrup
⅓ cup (65 g) brown sugar
⅓ cup (50 g) plain flour

½ tsp ground ginger
250 g mascarpone cheese
1 tbs icing sugar, plus extra to dust
1 tsp vanilla extract
200 ml cream, whipped

1 Preheat the oven to 180°C (160°C fan-forced). Lightly grease a baking tray, and line with non-stick baking paper. Spread the strawberries onto a plate or shallow dish and scatter with the caster sugar. Leave in a warm place for at least 20 minutes. They will become soft and release a delicious sweet juice.

2 In a saucepan over medium heat combine the butter, golden syrup and brown sugar and stir until melted. Set aside to cool, then stir in the flour and ginger.

3 Place small dollops (about 1½ teaspoons) of the mixture onto the baking tray, leaving plenty of space in between. You may fit only six per tray. Bake for 5 minutes and remove from the oven. Allow to cool for 2–3 minutes or until just starting to firm up.

4 Carefully lift them with a spatula and drape over small dariole moulds or glasses. Remove when they have cooled and hardened.

5 Using electric beaters, whip the mascarpone, icing sugar and vanilla until well combined. Fold through the whipped cream. Serve the brandy-snap baskets filled with the cream mixture, generously topped with strawberries and their juices. Sift icing sugar lightly over the top.

Chocolate mud cake

serves 12–16

Preparation time: 15 minutes
Cooking time: 1½ hours

The dense richness of this cake makes it a decadent dessert –
your guests would never guess how easy it is to make. For an extra kick,
exchange some of the coffee with bourbon or Tia Maria.

1¼ cups (310 ml) milk
250 g butter, cubed
2 cups (440 g) caster sugar
250 g dark cooking chocolate,
chopped or broken up
¼ cup (60 ml) strong black coffee (see Note)

1 tsp vanilla extract
1½ cups (225 g) plain flour
½ cup (75 g) self-raising flour
⅓ cup (35 g) cocoa powder
3 eggs, lightly beaten

1   Preheat the oven to 170°C (150°C fan-forced). Grease and line the base and sides of a 26 cm springform cake tin with non-stick baking paper.

2   In a medium saucepan combine the milk, butter, sugar, chocolate, coffee and vanilla extract. Stir over medium heat until melted together and smooth. Take off the heat to cool.

3   In a separate bowl sift the dry ingredients and make a well in the centre. When the chocolate mixture has cooled, pour it into the dry ingredients, stirring well. Add the eggs and stir again until well combined. The batter will be quite runny.

4   Pour the batter into the prepared tin and bake for 1½ hours, or until it comes away from the sides of the pan and is firm to a gentle touch in the centre. Cool in the tin for 10 minutes, then turn out onto a wire rack to cool completely before icing.

5   Ice with either a dark chocolate or cappuccino ganache (page 171).

Note: You can use 1 teaspoon of instant coffee dissolved in ¼ cup (60 ml) boiling water instead of brewed coffee.

Cappuccino ganache

makes enough for 1 cake

Preparation time: 5 minutes | Cooking time: 2 minutes + about 30 minutes cooling time

Something a little bit different – rich white chocolate and coffee flavoured ganache.

⅓ cup (80 ml) thickened cream
2 tsp instant coffee granules or powder

250 g white chocolate, grated
(or use white choc bits)

1   Place the cream into a microwave-safe jug or saucepan and heat to scalding point (almost boiling but not quite).

2   Stir in the instant coffee and mix well. Add the white chocolate and stir until the chocolate melts and the mixture is smooth.

3   Cool until the ganache is at room temperature and of a spreadable consistency. You can put it in the fridge but keep an eye on it so it doesn't become too hard. Use as is to ice a cake, or whip with electric beaters to make it fluffy.

Dark chocolate ganache

makes enough for 1 cake

Preparation time: 5 minutes | Cooking time: 2 minutes + about 30 minutes cooling time

Not only for icing cakes, this is great drizzled over ice cream or
as a dipping sauce for strawberries and bananas.

½ cup (125 ml) thickened cream

250 g dark chocolate, grated
(or use dark choc bits)

1   Place the cream into a microwave-safe jug or a small saucepan. Heat to scalding point – almost boiling but not quite. Add the chocolate and stir until the chocolate melts and the mixture is smooth.

2   Cool until the ganache is at room temperature and of a spreadable consistency, You can put it in the fridge but keep an eye on it so it doesn't become too hard. Use as is to ice a cake, or whip with electric beaters to make it fluffy.

Orange self-saucing puddings

serves 4

Preparation time: 15 minutes
Cooking time: 20 minutes

Self-saucing puddings hark back to olden times, are cheap to make
and wonderfully warming. They do need to be eaten straight away though,
or the sauce will be absorbed into the cake.

1¼ cups (190 g) self-raising flour
1¼ cups (275 g) caster sugar
3 oranges, zest finely grated, juiced
½ cup (125 ml) milk

1 egg
75 g butter, just melted
1 tbs cornflour

1   Preheat the oven to 170°C (150°C fan-forced), and lightly grease four 300 ml capacity ovenproof
ramekins. Stand them on an oven tray.

2   In a large bowl combine the flour, ½ cup (110 g) of the sugar and the orange zest. Whisk the milk,
egg and melted butter in a jug. Make a well in the flour and pour the wet ingredients into the dry
ingredients. Stir gently until combined. Spoon the batter into the prepared ramekins.

3   Combine ¾ cup (180 ml) water and the orange juice in a small saucepan. Bring to the boil for
1 minute, then remove from the heat. Combine the remaining sugar with the cornflour, and
sprinkle over the batter in each ramekin. Carefully pour the juice mixture over the top.

4   Bake for 20 minutes, or until the puddings are lightly golden on top and a skewer inserted into
the middle comes out clean. Serve hot with vanilla ice cream.

Golden syrup dumplings

serves 4–6

Preparation time: 15 minutes
Cooking time: 10 minutes

The first time I cooked for the three MasterChef judges at the auditions in Sydney,
Matt Preston asked me if I knew how to make golden syrup dumplings. I hadn't
made them before, but promised I would learn. I didn't get the chance to make them
during the competition (something tells me they wouldn't have been 'MasterCheffy' enough),
but here you go, Matt – golden syrup dumplings as requested.

1 cup (150 g) self-raising flour	**Syrup**
75 g butter, cubed, at room temperature	50 g butter
1 egg	1 cup (220 g) caster sugar
1 tsp water	½ cup (125 ml) golden syrup
	2 tbs lemon juice

1   Place the flour into a bowl and, using your fingertips, rub in the butter until the mixture looks like
breadcrumbs. Beat the egg with 1 tsp water and add to the flour. Stir with a butter knife until the
dough just comes together. It is important not to overwork the dough or the dumplings will be heavy
and tough. Divide the mixture into 24 balls (roughly teaspoonfuls).

2   In a large saucepan over medium heat combine the syrup ingredients with 2 cups (500 ml) water
and bring to a simmer. Drop the dumplings into the pan and cook for around 10 minutes. They will
be light and puffed up, and the sauce will thicken considerably. Serve hot with thick cream.

*'I learned a lot about cooking from studying Ayurveda. It teaches that the food
reflects the consciousness of the cook – in a lot of ways it is like a meditation. So when
I cook, the quality of my attention is reflected in the food. I love cooking for Andrea
because I know I am nourishing her with the love I put into it.' – Anthony*

7 | Heartland

'Heartland' is defined as 'the central region of a country or continent; especially a region that is important to a country or to a culture'. I would suggest that in a home where people are nourished and made welcome – whether they are family or friends or strangers – the kitchen is the home's heartland. It is central to the home's culture, to the landscape of the lives within.

This concept was most beautifully and simply expressed by Terese, the youngest of Grandma's eleven children. She remembers the heartland of her home and upbringing in these words:

'I have always thought that if I could have just one more day with my Mum it would be there in that kitchen at Cressy Road, watching her cook. I would "help" by licking the beaters or bowl, and be the official taste-tester. She was truly a marvel to watch in the kitchen and I don't know how she turned out all those cakes in such a short time – I don't think it was because of our help! I always felt that the kitchen was the heart of our home. The dining table was in there too, so it was where we sat to eat, to talk and do homework while Mum cooked dinner. To me that was the warmest place in the house – and I don't just mean because of the stove.'

The recipes in this chapter to me are 'heartland' recipes. They are not the necessities – not the daily fuel that we need for health and energy. Rather, these are the treats that are made when time is put aside just to cook for the joy of cooking and the pleasure of giving. They are made for the warm smell of sugar to work its magic, and bring a smile to the face of everyone who enters the house. This is the kind of cooking that Grandma's kids and grandkids reflect on most fondly when they are all grown up.

Sesame snap biscuits

makes about 40

Preparation time: 10 minutes + 15 minutes chilling
Cooking time: 10 minutes

These gorgeous biscuits are so easy to make.
If you love a hard, crunchy biscuit then this is the one for you!

1 cup (150 g) plain flour
1 tsp baking powder
1 cup (220 g) caster sugar
⅓ cup (50 g) sesame seeds

1 tsp salt
125 g butter, melted
¼ cup (60 ml) milk

1   Preheat oven to 220°C (200°C fan-forced) and line two large baking trays with non-stick baking paper. Combine the dry ingredients in a bowl. Pour in the melted butter and mix well, then add the milk and combine. The result will be a quite soft, sticky dough.

2   Lay a 40 cm piece of baking paper on the bench in front of you. Place the dough along the front edge in a sausage shape, about 4 cm in diameter and 20 cm long. Roll the baking paper up and twist the ends like a bonbon. Lay the package flat on a shelf in the freezer for 15–20 minutes or until firm.

3   Unwrap the package and slice the dough into 5 mm thick discs. Place on the baking tray, allowing space for spreading between each biscuit.

4   Place on two shelves of the oven for 10 minutes, swapping the trays at 5 minutes. Keep a very close eye on the biscuits – there are only moments between being done and being overdone, since the oven is so hot. When ready, the biscuits will be golden brown.

5   Remove the biscuits from the oven and allow them to cool for a couple of minutes on the tray before transferring to a wire rack. They will be very soft when they come out of the oven but harden up in a few minutes.

'When I was little I used to sneak out of bed and eat cookies in the middle of the night. I thought I was pretty stealthy but Mum would always come from nowhere and spring me.' – Josh

Monte Carlos

makes 12 large double biscuits

Preparation time: 15 minutes
Cooking time: 15 minutes

Mick's Grandma, Imelda, used to make these and they were always a part of the amazing assortment of baked goods that would appear on the table whenever guests came calling.

Biscuits
190 g butter, at room temperature
½ cup (100 g) brown sugar
1 egg
1 tsp vanilla extract
1 tbs honey
1 cup (150 g) self-raising flour
1 cup (150 g) plain flour

¾ cup (70 g) desiccated coconut
¼ cup (90 g) raspberry jam

Mock cream
60 g butter, at room temperature
¾ cup (110 g) icing mixture
½ tsp vanilla extract

1   Preheat the oven to 170°C (150°C fan-forced), and line a large baking tray with non-stick baking paper. Using electric beaters, beat the butter and sugar until pale and fluffy. Add the egg, vanilla and honey, and beat well again. Sift the flours into a separate bowl and stir in the coconut.

2   Using a wooden spoon, mix the dry ingredients with the butter mixture until it just comes together to form a dough. Handle the dough only as much as you need to, to bring it together.

3   Divide the mixture into 24 even pieces and roll into balls. Press into an oval shape on the prepared tray, and rough up the surface a little with a fork. Bake for 10–12 minutes or until golden brown. Cool for 10 minutes on the tray before transferring to a wire rack to cool completely.

4   To make the mock cream, beat the butter, icing mixture and vanilla together with electric beaters on high speed until light and fluffy. Add about 2 tablespoons of iced water a few drops at a time while beating constantly, until the mixture is white and glossy. Refrigerate for 15 minutes until the cream is firm.

5   Place a teaspoon of jam onto the flat side of 12 of the biscuits. Top with a large spoonful of mock cream and sandwich a second biscuit on top. Keep in an airtight container. In warm weather, store in the fridge.

Paddy's pecan and white choc chip cookies

makes about 36 cookies

Preparation time: 10 minutes
Cooking time: 12 minutes

In Paddy's last year of primary school, he would arrive home an hour before his brothers did, and have the kitchen to himself. During this time he experimented with cookies among other things, and we both agree that this particular invention was good enough to be shared.

185 g unsalted butter	2 cups (300 g) self-raising flour
1¼ cups (275 g) caster sugar	¼ tsp salt
1 egg	1 cup (120 g) pecans, roughly chopped
½ tsp vanilla essence	1⅓ cups (250 g) white choc bits

1   Preheat the oven to 180°C (160°C fan-forced). Line two large baking trays with non-stick baking paper. Using electric beaters, cream the butter and sugar until pale and fluffy, then beat in the egg and vanilla.

2   Gently mix in the sifted flour and the salt. Stir in the pecans and choc bits until evenly combined. Roll the mixture into balls about the size of a golf ball and place them on the prepared baking trays, about 6 cm apart to allow for spreading. Flatten them with a fork.

3   Bake for about 12 minutes. For a softer, chewy cookie get them out of the oven when they are just golden around the edges. For a crisper, lighter cookie, wait until they are golden all over.

4   Cool them on the trays for a couple of minutes until they firm up slightly, then transfer to a wire rack to cool completely. Store in an airtight container.

'I would love to be able to make cookies that are 95 per cent choc chips.' – Joe

*'We used to pick the mulberries from the tree behind the church.
Nan would take us home and whip up a delicious pie, which we
would eat for afternoon tea with a nice cuppa.' – Lyn*

Caramel slice

makes 20 squares

Preparation time: 20 minutes + cooling and refrigeration time
Cooking time: 40 minutes

Every school fete and cake stall in the country must have had a version of this
long-time favourite. I remember as a kid being disappointed if there was too much
biscuit base and not enough caramel – so this recipe has plenty of the good stuff and only
enough base to hold it all together. I hope it brings back some happy memories!

Biscuit base
½ cup (75 g) self-raising flour
½ cup (75 g) plain flour
¼ cup (20 g) desiccated coconut
¼ cup (50 g) brown sugar
80 g butter, melted

Caramel filling
4 x 395 g tins condensed milk
½ cup (125 ml) golden syrup
100 g butter

Topping
150 g dark chocolate, chopped
1 tbs vegetable oil

1   Preheat the oven to 180°C (160°C fan-forced). Grease a 26 x 17 cm slice tin and line the base with non-stick baking paper. Leave some baking paper hanging over the long sides of the pan to help lift the slice out.

2   In a large mixing bowl, combine the flours, coconut and brown sugar. Add the melted butter and mix well. Press mixture evenly into the base of the prepared tin, and bake 12–15 minutes or until golden. Set aside to cool.

3   In a large saucepan, place the condensed milk, golden syrup and butter into a saucepan and stir for 20 minutes over medium heat until mixture is light golden brown. Pour over the base and return to oven. Bake for 15 minutes, then set aside to cool.

4   When the caramel has cooled, melt the chocolate and oil in a small saucepan over low heat. Stir until smooth and well combined. Pour it over the caramel filling and spread to cover evenly. Refrigerate the slice for at least 3 hours before cutting into pieces with a sharp knife.

Vanilla slice

makes 12

Preparation time: 15 minutes
Cooking time: 25 minutes + chilling time

This involves a few different processes but is completely worth it.
Thick, cold vanilla custard, crispy pastry, passionfruit icing ... heaven.

2 sheets frozen puff pastry	½ cup (110 g) caster sugar
600 ml milk	⅓ cup (45 g) cornflour
1 lemon	50 g butter, cubed
1 vanilla pod, seeds scraped,	1½ cups (225 g) icing sugar mixture
or 1 teaspoon vanilla extract	pulp of 2 passionfruit
6 egg yolks	

1   Preheat the oven to 220ºC (200ºC fan-forced). Line two large baking trays with non-stick baking
paper. Allow the pastry to thaw slightly. Cut off a quarter from one side of each partially thawed pastry
sheet. Join onto the short end of each larger piece, pressing together and trimming to make a rectangle.
Place the rectangles onto a baking sheet and prick thoroughly with a fork. Bake for 20 minutes or until
golden brown. Remove the trays from the oven. Place one piece of pastry on top of the other and put
the empty tray on top. Place something heavy (like a couple of tins) on top of the baking tray.

2   Pour the milk into a saucepan. Using a vegetable peeler, peel 3 strips of rind from the lemon, avoiding
the white pith. Add the vanilla pod or extract. Bring slowly to the boil, then remove from the heat.

3   Meanwhile, beat the egg yolks and sugar with electric beaters until pale and thick. Add the cornflour
and beat again. Strain the milk and gradually pour it into the eggs, beating constantly. Return the
egg mixture to the saucepan and bring to the boil, beating with a wire whisk. The custard will thicken
considerably. Lower the heat a little and cook for a further 2–3 minutes, stirring all the while, and
making sure the custard does not catch and burn.

4   Remove from the heat and continue to beat with the wire whisk to release as much of the heat as
possible. When just warm, beat in the cubed butter.

5   Trim one pastry sheet to fit the bottom of a 25 cm x 16 cm lamington pan. Pour over the custard and
spread evenly. Trim the other pastry sheet to fit neatly on top, and place it upside down so it has a
smooth surface. Place in the fridge for at least an hour. Combine the icing sugar and passionfruit in
a bowl. When the slice has chilled, pour the icing over the top, spread out evenly and return to the
fridge for another half an hour. To serve, cut the slice into 12 pieces using a very sharp knife, taking
care to cut all the way through the bottom.

Fairy cakes

makes 24

Preparation time: 20 minutes
Cooking time: 15 minutes

These sweet treats are called fairy cakes because of their little wings, and how beautiful they are to look at. Perfect for a high tea or little girl's birthday party.

125 g butter	2 cups (300 g) self-raising flour
¾ cup (165 g) caster sugar	⅔ cup (160 ml) milk
1 tsp vanilla extract	600 ml thickened cream
2 eggs	2 tbs icing sugar
¼ tsp salt	⅓ cup (120 g) raspberry or strawberry jam

1 Preheat oven to 190ºC (170ºC fan-forced) and line two 12-hole cupcake trays with paper patty cases. Using electric beaters, beat the butter and sugar until pale and fluffy. Beat in the vanilla. Add the eggs one at a time and beat well after each one.

2 Fold through the salt and half the flour, followed by half the milk, then repeat with the remaining flour and milk. Handle the mixture gently, don't beat it too much or the cakes will be a bit chewy. Spoon into the patty cases, and bake for 10 minutes or until pale golden. Allow to cool completely.

3 Beat the cream and icing sugar with electric beaters until stiff peaks form. Put into a piping bag fitted with a 1 cm star nozzle. Cut the 'lids' off the cakes, and cut each lid in half. Pipe a generous swirl of cream onto the cut surface of the cake, and place the halves of the lid like wings. Alternatively, spoon the cream onto the cake. Place the jam into a small piping bag fitted with a 3 mm nozzle, and pipe a blob of jam in between the two wings. Alternatively, carefully drop the jam on with a teaspoon. Sprinkle with icing sugar.

'My favourite cooking memory is baking with Mum and licking the spoon.' – Bec

Lemon coconut cake

serves 8

Preparation time: 15 minutes
Cooking time: 35 minutes

This moist, dense cake has been a favourite in the Henebery family for years.

125 g unsalted butter, at room temperature
1 cup (220 g) caster sugar
2 eggs
½ cup (45 g) desiccated coconut
1 tbs lemon zest
1½ cups (225 g) self-raising flour
1 cup (250 ml) milk

Icing
1½ cups (225 g) icing mixture
1 cup (90 g) desiccated coconut
½ tsp finely grated lemon zest
¼ cup (60 ml) lemon juice

1 Pre-heat oven to 170°C (150°C fan-forced). Grease a 20 cm round cake tin and line the base with non-stick baking paper.

2 Using an electric mixer or electric hand beaters, cream the butter and sugar until light and fluffy. Add the eggs one at a time, beating well after each addition.

3 Stir in the coconut and lemon zest, then add half the flour and half the milk and stir through gently. Repeat with the remaining flour and milk.

4 Pour the batter into the prepared cake tin and bake for 35 minutes, or until golden and springy to a gentle touch. Turn out of the tin and cool completely on a wire rack.

5 For the icing, combine icing mixture, most of the coconut and the lemon zest with half of the lemon juice. Add the remaining lemon juice a little at a time until it is a spreadable consistency. Spread the icing over the cooled cake and sprinkle with remaining coconut.

'I like to cook for my work mates. I have quite a reputation for it and have people putting in their requests. Grandma's shortbread is always a hit, as well as her lemon coconut cake.' – Bec

Custardy apple cake

serves 8

Preparation time: 10 minutes
Cooking time: 1 hour

There's actually no custard in this cake, but the moist apples give it a
lovely custardy texture. This is a perfect afternoon tea treat.

2 eggs	¼ tsp cinnamon
1 cup (220 g) caster sugar	¼ tsp salt
125 g butter, melted	½ cup (125 ml) milk
1 tsp vanilla extract	4 Pink Lady or Granny Smith apples,
½ cup (75 g) self-raising flour	cored and thinly sliced

1   Preheat oven to 180°C (160°C fan-forced). Grease a 22 cm round cake tin and line the base with non-stick baking paper.

2   Beat the eggs in the bowl of an electric mixer until pale and creamy. Add the sugar and continue to beat for 5 minutes or until the mixture is thick and forms a ribbon. Stir in the butter and vanilla.

3   Add the flour, cinnamon, salt and milk, stirring through gently. Add the sliced apples and make sure all the apples are coated in the batter. The batter will be quite runny.

4   Pour into the cake tin and bake for one hour, or until golden brown, and coming slightly away from the sides of the pan. The cake is cooked when a skewer inserted into the centre comes out clean. Cool in the tin for 10 minutes before carefully turning out onto a wire rack. Dust with icing sugar and serve with thick cream.

'In my early high school years I loved cooking at home. I made rock cakes that were actually like rocks and sponge cake you could actually wipe up spills with.' – Tash

Treen's cherry ripe fudge cake

serves 12–16

Preparation time: 15 minutes
Cooking time: 1 hour

The moist, fudgy texture of the cake along with the cherries and coconut
make this cake even better to eat than its namesake chocolate bar.

250 g unsalted butter
200 g dark cooking chocolate, chopped
2 cups (440 g) caster sugar
2 tsp vanilla extract
400 ml tin coconut milk
1½ cups (225 g) plain flour
¼ cup (40 g) self-raising flour

¼ cup (25 g) cocoa powder
½ cup (40 g) shredded coconut, plus extra to
  decorate
1 tbs instant coffee (or 30 ml espresso coffee)
2 eggs, lightly beaten
200 g glacé cherries, chopped
dark chocolate ganache (page 171)

1 Preheat oven to 180°C (160°C fan-forced). Grease a 26 cm springform cake tin and line the base
   with non-stick baking paper.

2 Stir the butter, chocolate and caster sugar in a pan over medium heat until melted and smooth.
   Remove from the heat and stir in the vanilla. Add the coconut milk, stirring until well combined.
   Set aside to cool.

3 In a large bowl, combine all the dry ingredients. When the chocolate mixture has cooled, stir in
   the beaten egg, then stir it into the dry ingredients. Add one third of the chopped cherries and
   pour the batter into the tin. The batter should be quite runny. Sprinkle another third of the
   cherries over the top of the batter – they will sink in a bit.

4 Bake for 1 hour 15 minutes, or until the sides come away from the pan and the cake is firm
   but springy to touch. There will also be a lovely chocolate coconut smell. Let the cake stand
   for 10 minutes before turning out onto a wire rack to cool. Cool completely before icing.

5 Ice with dark chocolate ganache. Top with the remaining chopped cherries and
   extra coconut.

Pat's apple pie

serves 12

Preparation time: 30 minutes
Cooking time: 50 minutes

One afternoon my friend Mary rang me. She had made one of her mum Pat's famous apple pies and wanted to bring it around to share for afternoon tea. It was the best apple pie I had ever tasted. Pat uses whole cloves, but I prefer to use ground. Many thanks for your recipe, Pat!

Pastry	Filling
2 cups (300 g) plain flour	1.25 kg (5–6) Granny Smith apples, peeled, cored and finely sliced
¼ tsp salt	
½ cup (110 g) caster sugar	juice of 1 lemon
200 g butter, chopped	⅓ cup (75 g) caster sugar
1 egg	¼ tsp ground cinnamon
1 tbs cold water	¼ tsp ground cloves
	1 egg, lightly beaten
	1 tbs white sugar

1   Preheat the oven to 180ºC (160ºC fan-forced). Grease a pie dish or loose-based flan tin (25 cm base measurement). For the pastry, place the flour, salt, sugar and butter in a food processor and process in short bursts until a crumb texture is acquired. Add the egg and water and process again in short bursts until the mixture comes together.

2   Turn out onto a floured surface and knead briefly until the dough just comes together. Wrap in plastic wrap and place in the fridge for 15 minutes to chill.

3   For the filling, toss the apples with the lemon juice, sugar, cinnamon and cloves. Roll out two thirds of the pastry between two sheets of non-stick baking paper, and use to line the pie dish or flan tin. Prick with a fork and line with baking paper. Weigh the paper down with pastry weights or raw rice, and bake for 10 minutes. Remove from the oven and take out the baking paper and weights.

4   Place the apples into the pastry case. Roll out the remaining pastry and place on top of the apples. Press around the edges to seal, and cut some vents in the top. Brush the pastry with the egg combined with a splash of water and sprinkle with sugar. Bake for 40 minutes or until the crust is golden brown and cooked through.

5   Serve warm, with vanilla ice cream or double cream.

8 | Celebrate!

It's impossible to have a celebration without food. I state that categorically and with complete willingness to stand up and defend my position, no matter what foodless celebration examples are thrown at me. Food is at the heart of all of our most important days. Of course it is! It's the affirmation of life itself, it's the expression of generosity and abundance and love.

From the moment we start to plan a celebration, thoughts turn to what people will eat. Think of the lead-up to Christmas – who's bringing what? Who's getting the prawns? When are we getting together to make the puddings? Have you found any good mangoes?

Every special occasion demands a menu – a feast.

When I think back on the milestones of my life the standout moments are the celebrations. Christmases when Santa had to visit the tent because we were on a camping trip. The christenings of our sons, nieces and nephews, and the wonderful parties that followed. Birthdays, 21st parties, 40ths. Significant anniversaries. Engagement parties, graduation parties, weddings and even funerals – the celebration of a life passed. All of these celebrations mark the occasions that matter to me as a person, and to us as a family, a community and a culture.

The happiest celebration I can recall in my life is my wedding day. We had planned every detail with such care and excitement. The day was everything I had dreamed of since I was a little girl, and more. (As a little girl I didn't dream of boogying the night away to '80s hits.) We were surrounded by family and friends, food and wine, love and laughter and music. That celebration set the tone for our marriage – as it started, so it has continued, and we still love nothing more than an excuse to gather, to eat, to celebrate.

Easter roast lamb and gravy

serves 6–8

Preparation time: 5 minutes
Cooking time: 1½ hours

In many European countries it is traditional to eat roast lamb on Easter Sunday to celebrate. This is my nan's traditional roast lamb with the simplest gravy. It is just delicious.

2.5 kg lamb leg
3 garlic cloves, sliced lengthways
2 rosemary stems (about 12 cm long), leaves removed
salt and ground pepper

Old-fashioned gravy
¼ cup (40 g) plain flour
2 cups (500 ml) beef stock
salt and pepper

1　Preheat the oven to 180°C (160°C fan-forced). Using a small, sharp knife, pierce the lamb every 3 cm or so. Stuff each incision with a slice of garlic and a few rosemary leaves. Season the meat with salt and pepper.

2　Place into a roasting pan and roast for 1¼–1½ hours for medium. Remove from the oven and rest in the pan under foil for 30 minutes before carving.

3　After the roast has rested, transfer it to the carving board and leave under foil. If your roast was particularly fatty, ladle some of the fat out of the pan. Stir in the flour, ensuring there are no lumps. Place the pan over medium heat and introduce the beef stock little by little, stirring constantly. Bring to the boil, then taste and season. Pour into a serving jug.

Note: A rule of thumb for roasting lamb is to cook for 15 minutes, then 15 minutes per 500 g.

'Mum is very stubborn about having a baked dinner on Easter Sunday. One year we were living in a cottage while our house was being built. It had no oven but she borrowed someone else's. Another year we were in the middle of the bush and still had our pork roast. No matter what, she always finds a way.' – Joe

Rosemary roast potatoes

serves 4-6 as an accompaniment

Preparation time: 5 minutes
Cooking time: 25 minutes

The flavour of rosemary makes these a natural match for the Easter lamb.

600–700 g baby chat potatoes
50 g butter

1 tbs fresh rosemary leaves, chopped
sea salt flakes

1   Preheat oven to 200°C (180°C fan-forced). Place the potatoes, butter and rosemary into a non-stick baking dish.

2   Bake for 20–25 minutes, or until tender when pierced with a skewer (the time will depend on the size of the potatoes). Toss once or twice during cooking. Serve sprinkled with sea salt flakes.

Minted peas with feta

serves 4-6 as an accompaniment

Preparation time: 5 minutes
Cooking time: 6 minutes

Liven up plain baby peas with fresh mint and sharp feta.

500 g frozen baby peas
½ cup fresh mint leaves, shredded

100 g feta cheese, crumbled

1   In a microwave-safe container, place peas and cover with plastic wrap. Microwave on High for 6 minutes, or until heated through. Set aside, still covered.

2   Just before serving, toss through the mint and feta.

Hot cross buns

makes 12

Preparation time: 30 minutes + about 1 hour rising time
Cooking time: 25 minutes

Mick's grandma made her own hot cross buns every Easter, and as with everything she cooked they were so much better than the store-bought ones. I started making my own because Mick and Tom don't like sultanas – so I make some without for them. These are best eaten the day they are made, but can be brought back to life with a quick zap in the microwave or by toasting.

1¼ cups (310 ml) milk	1 tsp salt
¼ cup (55 g) caster sugar	60 g butter, at room temperature
2 x 8 g sachets dried yeast	1½ cups (250 g) sultanas
4 cups (600 g) plain flour	2 eggs, lightly beaten
2 tsp ground cinnamon	¼ cup (40 g) self-raising flour
2 tsp mixed spice	2 tbs apricot jam

1   In a microwave-safe jug, heat the milk for just over a minute or until warm. Add the caster sugar and stir until dissolved. Mix in the dried yeast. It is important at this stage that the milk is warm enough to activate the yeast but not too hot. Leave this mixture for 5–10 minutes or until it froths up a little.

2   In a large bowl, sift the flour, cinnamon, mixed spice and salt. Rub through the butter with your fingertips until it is evenly distributed. Stir through sultanas. Stir in the eggs and the yeast mixture with a wooden spoon until it comes together in a dough.

3   Turn out onto a floured work surface and knead by hand for 5 minutes until stretchy and smooth. Alternatively, place into the bowl of an electric mixer with the dough hook attachment and knead for 5 minutes. Place the dough in a large, greased bowl covered with plastic wrap. Place in a warm place for 45 minutes until it rises to almost twice its size. (If there are no warm or sunny spots in the kitchen, put the bowl under the range hood light.)

4   Preheat the oven to 180°C (160°C fan-forced). Knead the dough for a couple of minutes a second time, then divide into 12 balls. Place the balls onto a greased baking tray, pressed up against each other. Cover and leave in a warm place for another 15 minutes.

5   Combine the self-raising flour with two tablespoons of water and mix well. Place into a small piping bag with a narrow nozzle, or a plastic bag with a tiny piece of the corner snipped off. Pipe a cross onto each of the buns. Bake for 25 minutes, or until the buns have risen and sound hollow when tapped. Heat the jam with a little water in the microwave and brush over the hot buns to glaze.

Note: For tall hot cross buns, I put them into a greased 26 cm springform cake tin.

Jackie and Pete's stuffed Christmas turkey

serves 12

Preparation time: 30 minutes + overnight soaking
Cooking time: 3 hours

My friend Steph emigrated from England with her parents, Jackie and Pete,
and her brother Andrew when she was young. They have continued their tradition
of roasting a turkey, but give it an Aussie twist – it's done in the kettle barbecue!

1 size 60 turkey
1 cup (250 g) salt
2 cups (440 g) sugar

Stuffing
4 bunches parsley, leaves roughly chopped
(stalks discarded)

2 bunches sage, leaves roughly chopped
(stalks discarded)
2 kg brown onions, roughly chopped
2 loaves bread, crusts removed, torn
2 tsp salt
1 tsp freshly cracked black pepper
300 g butter, chopped

1 The night before cooking the turkey, mix the salt and sugar in a tub of water large enough for the turkey to be submerged. Put the turkey into the tub, and add plenty of large ice cubes (see Note). Leave it in the brine mixture overnight. Remove the turkey from the water at least an hour before cooking – pat dry and allow to come to room temperature.

2 Preheat the oven to 180°C (160°C fan-forced). Combine the parsley, sage and onions with ¼ cup water in a saucepan. Simmer over low heat for 10 minutes or until very soft. Drain well.

3 Process the bread to make very coarse crumbs, about the size of a fingernail. Any finer and the stuffing won't work. Combine the onion mixture with the breadcrumbs, salt and black pepper.

4 Clean the cavity of the bird with water and pat dry with paper towel. Place some of the stuffing in the cavity (enough to fill it loosely). Place the turkey into a large baking tray and bake for 3 hours. As juices collect in the baking tray, baste the breast. If wing tips or ends of the drumsticks start to colour too quickly, protect them with foil. The turkey is cooked when it is golden brown, the legs are loose in their joints and juices run clear when a skewer is inserted into the thickest part of the thigh meat. Remove any excess juices and reserve.

Continued next page ...

Celebrate!

Stuffed Christmas turkey *continued ...*

5 Meanwhile, pile the remaining stuffing into a shallow baking tray. Dot the chopped butter over the top and drizzle with 1 cup (250 ml) of the reserved turkey juices. Bake for 1½ hours. If the stuffing starts to dry out, add more juices. The end result should be moist, with a crunchy golden top. Rest the turkey, loosely covered with foil, for 30 minutes before serving with the extra stuffing and all the Christmas trimmings.

Note: Chances are your tub won't fit into the fridge, so my trick is to freeze water in small ice cream or takeaway containers to make giant ice cubes. The ice cubes take ages to defrost, but keeping them topped up means effectively keeping the turkey refrigerated in our hot climate! It's a bit of work but so worth it – it will be the most tender, moist turkey you have ever tasted. Another good trick is to use a large esky for this, if you have one. Take care that the turkey remains well chilled, so there are no food safety issues.

'One Christmas tradition that must be observed is wearing the paper hats out of the crackers. No hat, no eat.' – Steph

'For Christmas we always eat turkey with roast veg and made-from-scratch gravy, no matter what the weather. It's better now that Mum and Dad have air conditioning. Mum makes a huge amount of my Great-grandma's stuffing, so much so that it doesn't all fit into the bird and we have to cook some in a separate tray!' – Steph

Mum and Dad are as in
love today as they were
on their wedding day.

It was New Year's Eve 1978 and we were getting the house ready
for a big party. Dad was up a ladder hanging streamers. He thought
he had put up enough but the pink ones weren't up, so I whinged
and whined until, being the good patient Dad that he was, he
agreed to go up one more time and hang the pink ones. I was
excited and running around in circles, and one of my circles took
me right under the ladder. Nan nearly had a fit, saying it was bad
luck to walk under a ladder. I was patiently explaining to my nan
(in my wise 8-year-old way) that that was just a silly old wives'
tale – when the ladder came crashing to the ground. Dad broke
both his arms and the party went ahead while he and Mum were
at the hospital getting Dad's arms set in plaster. Dad still reckons
the worst part of it was getting back to the party and realising he
would have to drink his beer through a straw.

Sweet potato purée

serves 8 as an accompaniment

Preparation time: 5 minutes
Cooking time: about 10 minutes

This dish is lovely if the potatoes are roasted before puréeing, but I usually
have enough going on in the oven so this is a simple stove top recipe instead.

1 kg sweet potato   salt and ground white pepper
50 g butter   ground or freshly grated nutmeg

1   Peel the sweet potatoes and cut into similar-sized large chunks. Boil in a large pot of water until
    soft. Drain, and return to the pot. (Alternatively, steam in the microwave.)

2   Add the butter and purée with a hand-held blender. Add salt and pepper to taste and blend again.

3   This is able to be reheated – just add a little milk if it needs loosening up. Serve with nutmeg
    sprinkled over the top.

*'We always have a picnic tea at the beach with all the relatives on Boxing Day.
We bring our leftovers for tea and play Frisbee and footy. It's a wonderful
afternoon and evening which we all look forward to after the stresses that
can occur leading up to Christmas.' – Tash*

Pineapple glazed ham

serves as many people as you can invite over!

Preparation time: 15 minutes
Cooking time: 3 hours

If you haven't got room in your oven for a ham, it can be done in a barbecue with a hood.
It's lovely served either hot or cold.

7 kg leg of ham	½ cup (165 g) apricot jam
1½ cups (375 ml) pineapple juice	¼ cup (60 g) Dijon mustard
½ cup (100 g) brown sugar	¼ tsp salt

1   Preheat oven to 160°C (140°C fan-forced). Carefully remove the rind from the ham, leaving a good layer of fat intact. Leave rind around the shank of the leg. Score the fat in a diamond pattern, being careful not to cut all the way through to the meat or the fat will dislodge during cooking. Make a few deep incisions into the meat with a small sharp knife.

2   In a large saucepan combine the pineapple juice, brown sugar, jam, mustard and salt. Bring to the boil, and cook, stirring, for about 15 minutes, or until reduced to about 1⅓ cups (330 ml). The mixture will thicken as it cools and should have the consistency of a thick syrup. Be vigilant, as the mixture can bubble up to the brim of the pot. Allow to cool.

3   Baste the ham generously with the glaze, making sure that some gets into the deep incisions. Place the ham into a large baking dish and bake for 3 hours, basting with the marinade several times during cooking.

'At Christmas time when opening gifts we go from the youngest to the oldest one year, and the other way around the next year. Everyone can see what gifts have been given.' – Louise

Watermelon and feta salad

serves 8–10 as an accompaniment

Preparation time: 15 minutes

The red, green and white colours in this beautiful salad look like Christmas on a plate.
It's vibrant, refreshing, and perfect for our hot Aussie summer.

¼ ripe seedless watermelon, cut into 3 cm cubes
2 Lebanese cucumbers, seeded and sliced
  thinly on the diagonal
½ bunch shallots, very finely sliced

¼ cup mint leaves, coarsely chopped,
  plus some sprigs to serve
125 g feta
¼ cup (60 ml) white balsamic glaze (page 98)

1   Combine the watermelon, cucumber, shallots and mint in a large bowl and gently toss together.
    Arrange on a large white platter, and scatter with crumbled feta.

2   Drizzle the balsamic glaze over the salad, and serve with some mint sprigs on top.

Note: If you don't have white balsamic glaze on hand (either homemade or bought), you can use dark
balsamic glaze instead. The white version makes for a really beautiful presentation.

*'Last Christmas we had the family over for lunch and went all-out –
cold seafood platter, crusty bread, sauv blanc and Crown Lager.
It was easy to prepare and a magic day.' – Saul*

*'When I was six, my dad gave me an apron for Christmas. I cried and cried. Mum was
really annoyed with him – he gave my brothers bikes that year!' – Liane*

Pavlova roulade

serves 10–12

Preparation time: 20 minutes
Cooking time: 20 minutes

This dessert looks spectacular and is light enough to comfortably
follow a giant Christmas feast.

6 egg whites

1½ cups (330 g) caster sugar

1 tbs cornflour

1 tbs white vinegar

1 tsp vanilla extract

600 ml cream, whipped

2 punnets strawberries

1   Preheat the oven to 160°C (140° fan-forced). Grease and line a 26 x 34 cm baking tray with non-stick baking paper.

2   In the bowl of an electric mixer, beat the egg whites until soft peaks form. Add the sugar a little bit at a time, beating constantly, until the sugar is dissolved and stiff peaks form. Sprinkle over the cornflour, vinegar and vanilla and gently fold through the egg whites until combined. Do this very gently! Spread the mixture into the baking tray and bake for 20 minutes or until just firm. Meanwhile, slice half the strawberries and save the rest for serving.

3   When the meringue comes out of the oven, allow to cool for 5 minutes. Sprinkle a fresh sheet of baking paper with cornflour and lay it over the top of the meringue. Place a clean tea-towel on the bench, and carefully turn the baking dish upside down so that the meringue comes out on top of the baking paper/tea-towel. Carefully remove the baking paper from the bottom of the meringue. Spread half the cream in a line along the long edge of the meringue closest to you. Press the sliced strawberries into the cream.

4   Now the fun part – carefully, using the tea towel as a helping hand, roll the meringue over the cream until it looks like a log. Carefully lift onto a serving plate, putting the join at the bottom. Serve with remaining cream and strawberries.

Note: You can assemble the roulade up to 4 hours in advance, and refrigerate. It should be eaten the day it is made. If you like, spread remaining cream on top, and arrange quartered strawberries on the cream. Pomegranate seeds make a beautiful garnish.

White Christmas

makes 24 squares

Preparation time: 10 minutes
Cooking time: 2 minutes + 1–2 hours setting

I always thought this is what Bing Crosby was singing about – much better than snow in my opinion! This is a beautiful little gift if it's placed on a piece of gold or silver cardboard and wrapped with cellophane and a bow. Vary the fruit and nuts as you see fit.

1½ cups (75 g) mini marshmallows
2 cups (70 g) rice bubbles
1 cup (80 g) shredded coconut
1 cup (140 g) pistachio kernels, toasted and coarsely chopped

400 g white chocolate, chopped
(or white choc melts)
½ cup (75 g) dried apricots, chopped
½ cup (100 g) glacé cherries, chopped
½ cup (130 g) glacé pineapple, chopped

1   Grease a 20 x 30 cm lamington tin and line with non-stick baking paper, allowing a 5 cm overhang on the longer sides. Place the marshmallows, rice bubbles, coconut and pistachios into a bowl and mix well.

2   Melt the chocolate in a bowl over a saucepan of simmering water. Remove and stir into the dry ingredients, making sure it is thoroughly mixed. Add apricots, glacé cherries and pineapple, and mix quickly.

3   Tip into the tin and press out until evenly distributed. Cover with cling wrap and refrigerate 1–2 hours, before cutting into pieces.

Note: To toast the pistachios, spread onto an oven tray and cook in a preheated 180°C (160°C fan-forced) oven for 3–5 minutes, until fragrant and lightly coloured – keep an eye on them and take care not to burn.

'I have an annual ritual of making truffles. It's quite a long process but friends and family enjoy them and have come to expect them!' – Erin

Peanut brittle

makes a 25 x 15 cm slab

Preparation time: 2 minutes
Cooking time: 15 minutes

One of the characteristics of Christmas for me is the little dishes scattered about the house filled with festive treats – choc-coated almonds, pretzels, caramel popcorn, and this – gorgeous peanut brittle.

2 cups (440 g) white sugar   250 g salted, roasted peanuts
150 g unsalted butter

1   Line a baking tray with non-stick baking paper. Combine the sugar and butter with ¼ cup (60 ml) water in a large, heavy-based pan over medium-high heat. Bring to the boil, stirring gently to dissolve the sugar. Boil rapidly for 10–15 minutes, until the mixture turns a golden brown colour. Remove the pan from the heat and stir in the peanuts.

2   Working quickly, pour the mixture onto the tray and tilt to spread out. (Use a metal spoon to help it spread, if required.) The slab should be about the thickness of a peanut.

3   Place the tray somewhere cool and wait for the brittle to set. Shatter it into pieces and store in an airtight container.

'My Greek heritage has influenced the way I cook. When I am cooking for important celebrations I always prepare the traditional dishes I was brought up with.' – Maria

Birthday cake

serves 8–12

Preparation time: 15 minutes
Cooking time: 45 minutes

When we were little Mum used to always go to a huge amount of trouble to make
and decorate our birthday cakes. My best memories are of a beautiful butterfly cake,
a Humpty Dumpty sitting on a wall, and Debbie's coconut-covered teddy bear cake.
As I was born on Halloween, my 13th birthday was a Halloween dress-up party,
and my cake was in the shape of a ghost.

4 eggs	¼ tsp salt
2 cups (440 g) caster sugar	1 cup (250 ml) milk
2 cups (300 g) plain flour	125 g butter
2 tsp baking powder	1 tsp vanilla extract
	chocolate buttercream (see next page)

1 Preheat the oven to 160°C (140°C fan-forced). Grease two 20 cm round cake tins and line the base
with non-stick baking paper.

2 Using an electric mixer with a paddle attachment, beat the eggs for 4–5 minutes or until pale
and creamy. With the mixer still running, gradually add the caster sugar and continue to beat for
3–4 minutes. The mixture is ready when it 'forms the ribbon'. This means when the paddle or a
spoon is lifted out of the mixture, a trail is left across the surface for a moment before it sinks.

3 In a bowl, sift the flour, baking powder and salt. Add the egg mixture and fold through gently, until
just combined. Heat the milk, butter and the vanilla extract in the microwave or in a small saucepan
on the stovetop just until the butter has melted. Gently fold this through the batter, then pour into
the prepared tins.

4 Place the tins side by side on the centre shelf of the oven and bake for 45 minutes or until risen,
golden brown, and starting to come away from the sides of the tins. A skewer inserted into the
centre should come out clean. Cool in the tins for 10 minutes, then turn out onto a wire rack to cool
completely before icing with chocolate buttercream.

Chocolate buttercream

4 cups

Preparation time: 10 minutes

To make mocha buttercream, add 2 teaspoons of ground (not granular) instant coffee.

250 g unsalted butter, at room temperature
1 tsp vanilla extract
3 cups (450 g) pure icing sugar, sifted

½ cup (50 g) cocoa powder, sifted
¾ cup (180 ml) cream

1 Beat the butter and vanilla together with electric beaters until light and creamy. Decrease the speed and gradually add half of the icing sugar until completely incorporated.

2 Mix the cocoa powder and cream together until smooth. Add to the butter–sugar mixture in batches, alternating with the remaining icing sugar, until the buttercream is light and smooth.

'I loved Mum's Black Forest cake, and requested it every birthday.' – Michelle

'Kieron made a layer cake for my 34th birthday. It had so many layers it was nearly a foot high and one slice took nearly an entire dinner plate – it was a meal in itself!' – Deb

We spent most of our Christmases on the South Coast in a tent when we were little and later in Nan's holiday cottage. If the moon was right, we would go prawning and catch school prawns with hand nets. We also had a lobster pot, which Dad put in the ocean off the headland. We weren't rich by any means but we certainly felt rich when there were fresh prawns and lobster to go with the Christmas ham.

Dad and his lobster!

Almond bread

makes approx 35 slices

Preparation time: 5 minutes
Cooking time: 45 minutes

Almonds are particularly significant in Greek, Italian and Middle Eastern weddings. Traditionally, five sugared almonds are given to wedding guests, to symbolise happiness, health, wealth, children and longevity.

3 egg whites
½ cup (110 g) caster sugar
½ tsp vanilla extract

½ cup (75 g) plain flour
100 g unblanched almonds (with skins on)

1   Preheat the oven to 180°C (160°C fan-forced). Grease a 25 cm x 7 cm x 4 cm bar tin, and line with non-stick baking paper, allowing some overhang on the two long sides.

2   Using electric beaters, beat the egg whites in a clean bowl until doubled in volume and stiff peaks form. Gradually add the sugar, a little at a time, until all incorporated.

3   Using a spatula or large metal spoon, fold through vanilla extract, flour and almonds. Spoon into the prepared tin, and bake for 35–40 minutes or until a skewer inserted into the cake comes out clean. Cool on a wire rack until completely cold. Wrap loaf in foil and refrigerate overnight.

4   Preheat the oven to 160°C (140°C fan-forced) and line two baking trays with non-stick baking paper. Using a serrated knife, carefully cut the loaf into thin slices. Place in a single layer on the trays. Bake for 20 minutes, or until the almond bread is crisp and hardened but not browned. Cool completely before storing in an airtight container.

'The best wedding I have ever been to was my own. We didn't have much money. It was at the local RSL – good food, excellent company, and much dancing and laughter.' – Alison

2

: Nut Loaf :-

5 Tablespoons S. R. Flour sift with
a pinch salt
1 dessertspoonful brown sugar, Break about
2 teaspoonfuls good fat into this & rub
in fine texture.
1/2 cup chopped nuts & 1 egg
1 dessertspoonful golden Syrup with
1/2 cup milk & add gradually to mixture make
a slightly slack mixture.

" Ginger Loaf :-

2 cups S. R. Flour
1 cup Sugar
1 cup Sliced Ginger
1 teaspoon Cocoa
1 teaspoon Butter
1 egg.
3/4 cup milk.

: Method :-

Sift flour & cocoa, rub in butter, add sugar & ginger
now mix into a dough with the beaten egg & milk.
Pour into a loaf tin & bake in moderate oven
40 to 45 mins.

9 | *The heart of our home*

Who, or what, is the heart of your home?

I asked this question dozens of times when writing this book. The answers were sometimes unexpected, sometimes funny, sometimes warming. It made me think about the heart of my home and opened the floodgates for many beautiful memories.

This blank chapter is for you to record what makes your family special. What recipes, stories, photographs; what handwritten snippets from generations past or favourite clippings from magazines; what favourite quotes or pieces of wisdom you may want to pass forward.

Sometimes when faced with a blank notebook I freeze, thinking that whatever I put down can't be worthy of the pristine new pages. And so, often they remain blank. I would encourage you to grab a pen and just get started. The following pages are not worth anything until they contain your journey.

Who, or what, is the heart of your home?

Acknowledgements

I am still pinching myself about the good fortune that has allowed me to write another cookbook. *The Heart of the Home* has been as much a learning curve for me as *Our Family Table*, and again there is a major team behind the scenes making sure everything works.

I would like to thank the team at Random House Australia – Nikki Christer, Nikla Martin, Anna Govender – for their talent, advice and patience, and to designer Jay Ryves at Future Classic.

Thanks again to the wonderful food team – I am so thrilled to have been able to work with you again. Tracy Rutherford, recipe editor extraordinaire; Nick Eade, true master chef; Janelle Bloom, beautiful stylist and lady; and Steve Brown, transcendent photographer – thanks to you all for being so, so good at what you do and such a joy to work with.

To Lisa Sullivan and Caitlin Sullivan from One Management, thanks for being my trusted advisors and for always having my back.

To each person who contributed their thoughts, stories and recipes for this book, an enormous thank you. Everyone has been so generous with their time, allowing me insights into many different situations, cultures and attitudes.

Since the MasterChef experience I have had the privilege of meeting so many fabulous chefs and cooks who have shared their secrets, invited me into their kitchens and inspired me with their knowledge and creativity. In a very real way you have all contributed to my growing and learning, and I thank you.

To my biggest taste testers and most enthusiastic recipients of my cooking – my dear friends and family – thanks for giving me excuse after excuse to get into the kitchen, cook my heart out and celebrate life with you all.

Joe, Tom and Paddy, thank you for keeping my feet on the ground, for your total and unconditional love, for being so willing to join in the adventure, and for filling our house with laughter every single day.

Mick, thank you for being my heart, my soul and my life.

Index

ENJOY

An Ebury Press book
Published by Random House Australia Pty Ltd

Level 3, 100 Pacific Highway, North Sydney NSW 2060
www.randomhouse.com.au

First published by Ebury Press in 2011

Addresses for companies within the Random house Group
can be found at www.randomhouse.com.au/offices

National Library of Australia
Cataloguing-in-Publication Entry
Author: Goodwin, Julie.
Title: The Heart of the Home / Julie Goodwin
ISBN: 978 1 74275 009 5 (hbk).
Subjects: Cooking.
641.5

Cover and internals designed by Jay Ryves and Naomi Solomon, Future Classic
Edited by Tracy Rutherford
Food styling by Janelle Bloom
Photography by Steve Brown
Index by Puddingburn Publishing Services
Printed and bound by Everbest Printing Co Ltd. Printed in China.

The publishers would like to thank www.paper2.com.au, House, Village Living, Kmart and Ikea for the wonderful paper, stationery, crockery, cutlery and bakeware used throughout this book.